Documents and Debates
Bismarck and German Unification

Documents and Debates
General Editor: John Wroughton MA., F.R.Hist.S.

Bismarck and German Unification

David Hargreaves

Assistant Master, Westminster School

MACMILLAN

First published 1991

Published by
MACMILLAN EDUCATION LTD
Houndmills, Basingstoke, Hampshire RG21 2XS
and London
Companies and representatives
throughout the world

Typeset by Footnote Graphics, Warminster, Wiltshire

Printed in Hong Kong

British Library Cataloguing in Publication Data
Hargreaves, David *1959–*
Bismarck and German unification. – (Documents and
debates).
1. Germany. Political events. Role of Bismarck, Otto Furst
von
I. Title II. Series
943.081092
ISBN 0–333–53775–0

For Harry

Contents

General Editor's Preface

This book forms part of a series entitled *Documents and Debates*, which is aimed primarily at sixth formers. The earlier volumes in the series each covered approximately one century of history, using material both from original documents and from modern historians. The more recent volumes, however, are designed in response to the changing trends in history examinations at 18 plus, most of which now demand the study of documentary sources and the testing of historical skills. Each volume therefore concentrates on a particular topic within a narrower span of time. It consists of eight sections, each dealing with a major theme in depth, illustrated by extracts drawn from primary sources. The series intends partly to provide experience for those pupils who are required to answer questions on documentary material at A-level, and partly to provide pupils of all abilities with a digestible and interesting collection of source material, which will extend the normal textbook approach.

This book is designed essentially for the pupil's own personal use. The author's introduction will put the period as a whole into perspective, highlighting the central issues, main controversies, available source material and recent developments. Although it is clearly not our intention to replace the traditional textbook, each section will carry its own brief introduction, which will set the documents into context. A wide variety of source material has been used in order to give the pupils the maximum amount of experience – letters, speeches, newspapers, memoirs, diaries, official papers, Acts of Parliament, Minute Books, accounts, local documents, family papers, etc. The questions vary in difficulty, but aim throughout to compel the pupil to think in depth by the use of unfamiliar material. Historical knowledge and understanding will be tested, as well as basic comprehension. Pupils will also be encouraged by the questions to assess the reliability of evidence, to recognise bias and emotional prejudice, to reconcile conflicting accounts and to extract the essential from the irrelevant. Some questions, *marked with an asterisk*, require knowledge outside the immediate extract and are intended for further research or discussion, based on the pupil's general knowledge of the period. Finally, we hope that students using this material will learn something of the nature of historical inquiry and the role of the historian.

John Wroughton

Acknowledgements

The author and publishers wish to thank the following for permission to use copyright material:

Oxford University Press for extracts from Helmut Böhme, *The Foundation of the German Empire*, translator, Agatha Ramm, 1971; Rutgers University Press for extracts from *Documents of German History*, edited by Louis L. Snyder, copyright © 1958 by Rutgers, The State University.

Every effort has been made to trace all the copyright holders, but if any have been inadvertently overlooked the publishers will be pleased to make the necessary arrangement at the first opportunity.

General Introduction

The purpose of using, almost exclusively, original source material to study Bismarck and the story of German unification may need explaining. It is an area of history which suffers unusually from potent myths and half truths, many of these fostered by Bismarck himself. Palmer's biography of Bismarck calculates over 6,000 books and academic articles written about him. And, although the Revisionist School has gone a long way (too far for many tastes) in seeking to qualify Bismarck's role in German unification, he still bestrides the subject as a colossus who somehow cannot go away.

For the non-Germanist, the translated sources readily available are somewhat limited. Helmut Böhme's *The Foundation of the German Empire* (1971) is a classic anthology of mainly political source material, translated by Agatha Ramm which has been wholly indispensable in the writing of this book, *From Bismarck to Hitler: the Problem of Continuity in German History* ed. J. C. Röhl, (Longman, 1970), *Germany in the Age of Bismarck* ed. W. M. Simon (Allen & Unwin, 1968), *Documents of German History* ed. L. L. Snyder (Rutgers University Press, 1958) have all also been especially useful here. Also helpful are *The Age of Bismarck, Documents and Interpretations* (Harper Row, 1973) and *The Social Foundations of German Unification*, 1858–1871 (Princeton, 1969) both by T. S. Hamerow. *Bismarck and Europe* eds W. N. Medlicott and D. K. Coveney (Edward Arnold, 1971) is an excellent reference source. For reminiscences, Bismarck's own *Bismarck, the Man and Statesman, being the reflections and reminiscences of Otto Prince von Bismarck* (trans. A. J. Butler (Smith Elder, 1898) remains a risky but entertaining source of enlightenment.

The chapters in this book are essentially chronological. This was a decision imposed by historical common sense after 1848, and especially after 1861, when the pace and pressure of events becomes so rapid, and the assumptions of politics (national and foreign) so repeatedly challenged that each phase requires separate scrutiny. Historians, of course, invent 'phases' even where they do not find them, but in this case such subterfuge was not necessary. Bismarck's turbulent coming to power, the war with Denmark and the uneasy peace with Austria, the Seven Weeks' War and the creation of the North German Confederation, the attempts to forge a closer relationship with the southern states in Germany and the explosion of war with France – all these marked separate and distinctive episodes. By taking the first two chapters to deal with the idea of German unity well in advance of Bismarck's premiership, an effort has been made to underline the conviction – reinforced overwhelmingly in the selection of source material printed here – that German unification was an important issue long before Bismarck seized it.

A close scrutiny of the primary source material, while it will certainly not resolve the controversy over German unification, has at least the merit of sharpening the student's *perceptions*. One reads Bismarck's speeches to the *Reichstag*, his letters to the king, his submissions to the Royal Council, and gathers snatches of table talk with his wife and family. In none of these situations can we be assured of his spontaneity, but we can at least see what some of his preoccupations were, and how he chose to articulate them. The same, of course, is entirely true of his statesmen contemporaries, friends or adversaries, and their perceptions of him – while quite as often contrived for an audience – can only quicken the historian's instinct. From the plethora of correspondence, minutes and miscellany of other records of Bismarck's career during his premiership between 1861 and 1871, one conviction above all may crystallise: that he was a man above all addicted to making what he would of the moment, an improviser whose political convictions were instinctive rather than intellectual. As befits a committed politician, his interest was in the acquisition of power; in his deployment of it, he was always far more diffident. His only reference point was whether or not any particular course of action would damage what he conceived of as his interests.

This is not at all to say that the sources convict Bismarck of megalomania, at least not until 1871. Rather, they point to his limited role. Foreign statesmen, particularly Count Rechberg from Austria, were sceptical about the honesty of Prussian intentions long before Bismarck was singled out by King William I. Once Bismarck came to power, it is clear from the political minutiae that he was *busy*. Unlike the future German Führer, Adolf Hitler, the political preconditions for whom he has often been blamed for helping to create, Bismarck was both very hard-worked and entirely accountable. In his most famous speech to the *Landtag* in 1862, with its notorious reference to 'blood and iron', in his manipulation of the constitution of the North German Confederation, in his distressed exchanges with the king over the imperial style he (William) was to be accorded, it is Bismarck's frank delight in politics, his preoccupation at somehow wangling his way through antagonistic forces which comes across. He was an upmarket Mr Fixit, and not a self-conscious Rambo. Whatever damage his political legacy did to Germany, a close scrutiny of the primary material may lead one to view him more benignly than otherwise.

Many of the controversies involving German unification revolve around Bismarck: his own garrulous memoirs saw to that, and one can speculate that, in his pique, he may have taken considerable satisfaction in laying historical 'landmines' for his future biographers. While it is germane to our understanding to decide his intentions in allying with Austria against the Danes, or in the benign treatment he accorded the Austrians after Konnigratz, and to what extent he wished to provoke war with France after 1867, it is too easy to confuse these with the essential controversy of German unification itself. If scrutiny of primary material leaves us undecided on all else, it does at least prove unequivocally that well in advance of Bismarck, the issue of national unification evoked vitality and concern. The passionate nature of the speakers at the Wartburg Festival in 1817 may seem to tell us little more than that students then, as later, espoused ideas with a romanticism and conviction matched only by their naivety. But the call for German unity – the precise nature of which was enticingly unclear – was also a call to assuage wounded pride in the wake of Napoleonic invasion. It also accorded well with emergent mercantile and industrial interests seeking a demolition of restrictive tariff barriers. However little appeal the hot-headed actions of students may have held, national unity had emotional resonance and practical advantages which cut right across class and even the cultural divide among the different states in the Confederation.

Prussia's role in all this is highly elusive. There is no doubt that she felt herself a thwarted power. The antagonism of Europe in general since the days of Frederick II had dulled but had never evaporated. Her defeat at Jena and the snub (as she saw it) of Austria's Presidency of the German Confederation made her perceptibly more disgruntled with the *status quo* than other states. The critical device in this was of course her increasing wealth and economic authority, enshrined in the *Zollverein*. Yet, as elections in south Germany to the Customs Parliament in 1868 resoundingly proved, Austria and not Germany was the more trusted of the great German powers. What does all this suggest? That Prussia was predestined to govern Germany? That Bismarck was predestined to manage that government? Surely not. The critical and enduring conditions here was the sense of vulnerability of the smaller states in Germany and the relentless pressure of powerful interest groups, often in the ascendant, to orchestrate the creation of *kleindeutschland*.

The sources largely deal with (and emanate from) the powerful. Yet among the powerful, there was a curious dichotomy which becomes increasingly apparent the more one delves into the material. The forces of the old world and the new in an increasingly doubtful equilibrium suggest that, Bismarck or no Bismarck, *Vorparlament* or not, the German Confederation was a fudge dreamed up by an *ancien régime*. It presupposed a world of small German states, of thoroughly unconstitutional monarchs, and of an enduringly and pre-eminently strong Austria. It was a pastoral vision, and therein lay its flaw. While it is absolutely true that the Confederation was dismantled by Bismarck and the nineteenth century phenomenon of popular nationalism, it was first and foremost destroyed by industrialisation, by urbanisation and the profound social dislocation these engendered at all levels of society. To read for instance the correspondence of Louis II of Bavaria in the later 1860s is to read the hand-wringing vapourings of an old man whose day has long passed; he evidently had not realised it but one may sense his audience averting their eyes in embarrassment.

A thought, and a doubt, remain at the end of these sources. German unification had critically different connotations for its supporters. An economic gravy train for some, a harbinger of military excellence for others, the recreation of a mythical bygone Golden Age, a Prussian triumph, an obscure sense of righting past wrongs – each of these visions had its adherents. Yet as Bismarck prepared the new constitution in 1871 for the Second Reich, one wonders whether or not he knew that historians would one day hotly dispute the nature of his success. Prussia into Germany or Germany into Prussia? However united people were in the *demand* for German unification, such consensus certainly did not extend to its *meaning*. The cost of that, however, would be measured after 1871 when even Bismarck showed signs of finding the consequences of victory (his victory indeed) at times vexatious and hollow.

I In the Shadow of Napoleon: the German Confederation, 1815–1848

The move towards unification in Germany received, intentionally or otherwise, an enormous fillip through the Congress of Vienna. Germany lacked coherent, defensible frontiers and this undoubtedly contributed to a perennial sense of insecurity. At the Congress of Vienna in 1815 her 16 separate states (until 1806 there had been over 200) were incorporated into the German Confederation. It was no more than a token attempt at union: Austria was evidently determined to assert her pre-eminence though her own population was far too heterogeneous for her to feel comfortable with any formal statement of the national principle. Instead, she led the way in paying pious regard to the amorphous Confederation and vehemently opposing change which compromised her autonomy. The need to obtain a two-thirds vote in the *Diet* before passing any substantial measure effectively reduced it to impotence.

This suited Austria exactly: she did not seek to challenge the profound cultural separatism of the different German states – indeed she relied upon it as a part of the *status quo* she sought to preserve. Her reactions to change tended to be choleric, as Metternich's Carlsbad Decrees (issued in the wake of the Wartburg Festival) showed. This intolerant response was typical enough in central or eastern Europe at this time, and was certainly of a piece with the 'Holy Alliance' precepts favoured by the Tsar and Emperor of Austria at this time.

But, as a style, it was too provocative to soothe domestic opinion and too defensive to deter foreign critics. Protest, even rioting, was perennial in the early years of the German Confederation, usually on a local scale. In 1832 both Austria and Prussia used the *Diet* at Frankfurt to pass the so-called Six Acts, curbing the press and strengthening the powers of princes against those of parliamentary assemblies. The Prussian government was acutely suspicious of Austrian designs, but their rivalry was essentially a question of who was to exercise *control* over German affairs, rather than one of style.

To wrest control in the longer term, she sought the initiative in the short term. Prussia's industrial and economic sophistication before 1850 should not be exaggerated; it was only then that her position of advantage *vis-à-vis* Austria became pronounced. But, borrowing the ideas of Friedrich List of Württemberg, the Prussian government orchestrated the creation of the *Zollverein* and led it. The thinking at this stage was primarily defensive – to pre-empt any Austrian attempts to suborn the economies of smaller German states through her presidency of the Confederation. Certainly, in 1834, the Prussian government's commitment to free trade was qualified: it was an economic convenience (strictly within the parameters of its membership) and it served to disadvantage Austria. That hardly amounted to plans for national unification. Metternich might baulk at this, but until 1848 Austrian apprehensions concerning Prussia's power were controlled. Economically, whatever the truth of the gap opening between the two states, the threat posed by Prussia simply was not generally perceived by the other side.

A range of domestic controversies (political as well as economic) saw the explosion of trouble in Berlin, as well as in Vienna (and other Austrian capitals) in 1848. Tension between Austria and Prussia was not primarily what these were about. The Frankfurt National Parliament represented the intellectual middle-class protest in Berlin, not by any stretch an emergent proletariat, whom it rapidly disowned, and was properly marginalised by reactionary and commercial interests. Yet 1848 was perhaps to be the *annus mirabilis* for German unification, if not for the reasons suggested by romantic versions of the nationalist story. After 1848, Austria had been challenged – variously, and for a time successfully. Her frontiers were patently too long, her population too mixed, her resources too stretched. The Frankfurt parliament was a crude fusion of incompatible ideas, but it is no coincidence that this challenge to the Austrian-dominated Confederation occurred the year that Austria, above all, faced extraordinary assaults. Very little of the spirit of the Frankfurt parliament, indeed, remained – but the memory of Austrian vulnerability would not be so easily lost.

1   The Creation of the German Confederation

The sovereign princes and the free towns of Germany . . . convinced of the advantages which would accrue for the security and independence of Germany and for the well-being and equilibrium of Europe from a strong and lasting union, have agreed to unite
5   themselves in a perpetual confederation, and, for this reason, have given their representatives and envoys at the Congress of Vienna full powers . . . .

Article 1. The sovereign princes and the free towns of Germany, including their Majesties the Emperor of Austria and the Kings of
10   Prussia, Denmark and the Netherlands – the Emperor of Austria and the King of Prussia because of their possessions formerly belonging to the German Empire; the King of Denmark for

Holstein; and the King of the Netherlands for the Grand Duchy of Luxembourg – unite in a perpetual union which shall be called the
15 German Confederation.

Article 2. The aim ... shall be the maintenance of the external and internal security of Germany as well as the independence and inviolability of the individual German states.

Article 3. All members of the Confederation shall have equal
20 rights. They all agree to maintain the Act of Confederation.

Article 4. The affairs of the Confederation shall be managed by a *Diet* of the Confederation, in which all members of the Confederation shall vote through their representatives, either individually or collectively ... without prejudice to their rank ....

25 Article 5. Austria shall preside over the *Diet* of the Confederation. Each member of the Confederation shall have the right to initiate and support proposals. Austria as the presiding state is bound within a given period to bring these proposals to deliberation.

30 Article 6. When fundamental laws of the Confederation are to be enacted or amended ... the *Diet* shall exist as a general assembly, in which the distribution of the votes [shall be] based upon the geographical extent of the individual states ....

35 Article 11. All members of the Confederation pledge themselves to protect Germany as a whole, and also every single confederated state, against attack ... If war is declared by the Confederation, no individual member may negotiate separately with the enemy, conclude an armistice, or make peace.

40 Article 12. The members of the Confederation reserve to themselves the right of forming alliances of any kind. However they pledge themselves to make no commitments that shall be directed against the security of the Confederation or any individual state within it.

P. A. G. von Meyer (1833) *Corpus juris confederationis Germanicae*, quoted in L. L. Snyder (1958) *Documents of German History* (Rutgers University Press)

Questions

★ a What was happening at the Congress of Vienna (line 6)?
★ b What were the 'free towns of Germany' (line 1)?
  c Comment on the idea of 'equal rights for all members of the Confederation' (lines 19–20) in the light of other clauses in the agreement.
  d Explain the function of the *Diet* in the Confederation.
  e What was the significance of Austria's presidency of the Confederation (lines 25–29)?
  f What is to be understood by 'fundamental laws' (line 30)?
★ g Under what circumstances might Article 11 and Article 12 seem wishful thinking rather than political reality?

2   The Wartburg Festival, 1817

On the 19th at nine in the morning the students, who had
assembled in the market place, marched to the castle, banners and a
band at their head. We accompanied them. ... When general
silence was obtained, a student delivered a speech on very much
5   the following lines: he spoke of the aim of this assembly of
educated young men of all circles and all races of the German
fatherland: of the thwarted life of the past; of the rebound, and the
ideal that now possessed the German people; of hopes that had
failed and been deceived; of the vocation of the student and the
10   legitimate expectations which the Fatherland founded upon it; of
the destitution and even persecution to which a youth devoting
himself to science had to submit; finally, how they must themselves
take thought to introduce among them order, rule and custom. ...
The audience, and we men among them, were moved to tears,
15   tears of shame that we had not so acted, of pain in that we were
the cause of so much distress, of joy over this intellectual
message. ...

   In one of the groups a speech of the following tenor was
delivered: 'Dear friends, you must not let this movement of
20   emotion and exaltation pass in smoke. It will not return. Now or
never must you be united. You must not let the matter rest at mere
emotion, you must not allow any one to depart from the Wartburg
Festival without talking some real possession. ... What have we
gained? Are our relations different from what they were before?
25   Are the 'nations' dissolved? Are we members of a greater society?
Does each of us only represent the students' union of his individual
university, or do we together form branches of a universal German
Student's Union?

   '... Let your name be what you are alone and exclusively,
30   namely, the Students' Union or the League of Youth. ... But be on
your guard against wearing a badge and so sinking to party
distinctions, proof that you do not realise that the status of the
educated class reproduces in itself the whole state, and therefore
destroys its being by breaking up into parties. ... Germany
35   depends only on itself, on Germany as a whole. ... Yours is not to
discuss what should or should not happen in the state; what alone
is seemly for you to consider is, what your business shall one day
be in the state, and how you can prepare yourselves to be fit for
it. ...'

40   Afterwards, trial by fire was held over the following articles,
which were first displayed high in the air on a pitchfork to the
assembled multitude, and then with curses hurled into the flames.
The articles burnt were these: a bagwig, a guardsman's stays, a
corporal's cane. ...

45   ... Many of those who manage the affairs of Germany, and still

more, those who mismanage them, might well take the conclave
at the Wartburg as an example.

> J. G. Legge (1918) *Rhyme and Revolution in Germany* (London), pp 21–25, quoted in L. L. Snyder *op. cit.*

Questions

a What is to be understood by 'the thwarted life of the past' (line 7)?
b Comment on the nature of the portrayal of a student given in this passage.
c 'Be on your guard against ... sinking to party distinctions' (lines 30–32). In what way does this statement suggest limited vision on the part of the speaker?
d Is the vision outlined in this passage fundamentally liberal or authoritarian? Explain your answer.
★ e How seriously do you imagine the rulers of Germany took the warnings of the writer delivered in the last paragraph?

3   The Carlsbad Decrees of 1819

1. There shall be appointed for each university a special representative of the ruler of each state, the said representative to have appropriate instructions and extended powers. . . . This representative shall enforce strictly the existing laws and disciplinary regula-
5 tions; he shall observe with care the attitude shown by the university instructors in their public lectures and registered courses; and he shall, without directly interfering in scientific matters or in teaching methods, give a beneficial direction to the teaching, keeping in view the future attitude of the students. Finally, he shall give
10 unceasing attention to everything that may promote morality. . . .
2. The Confederated governments mutually pledge themselves to eliminate from the universities . . . all instructors who shall have obviously proved their unfitness for the important work entrusted to them by . . . abusing their legitimate influence over young
15 minds, or by presenting harmful ideas hostile to public order or subverting existing governmental instructions. . . .
3. The laws that for some time have been directed against secret and unauthorised societies in the universities shall be strictly enforced. . . . The special representatives of the government are
20 enjoined to exert great care in watching these organisations. . . .
4. No student who shall have been expelled from any university by virtue of a decision of the university senate . . . shall be admitted to any other university.
i. As long as this edict remains in force, no publication . . . shall
25 be printed in any state of the Confederation, without the prior knowledge and approval of the state officials. . . .

iv. Each state of the Confederation is responsible, not only to the state against which the offence is directly committed but to the entire Confederation. . . .

> P. A. G. Meyer *Corpus juris Confederationis Germanicae*, vol II, pp 138ff quoted in L. L. Snyder (1958) *Documents of German History* (Rutgers University Press)

Questions

a In what respect does the need for the Carlsbad Decrees corroborate the prognosis of the writer in the second passage?

b Comment on 'the beneficial direction to teaching' suggested in line 8.

c What conception of 'morality' (line 10) is gained from this extract?

★ *d* Which of the decrees would you suppose to have been most alarming and immediately significant for those likely to have been affected by them?

e How far did these decrees in fact represent the wish of the German Confederation? If not theirs, whose?

4   The creation of the *Zollverein*

(i) I was led to consider the nature of *nationality*. I perceived that the popular theory took no account of *nations*, but simply of the entire human race on the one hand, or of single individuals on the other. I saw clearly that free competition between two nations

5   which are highly civilised can be mutually beneficial only in case both of them are in a nearly equal position of industrial development, and that any nation which, owing to misfortunes, is getting behind others in industry, commerce and navigation, must first of all strengthen its own individual powers. . . . I felt that Germany

10 must abolish her internal tariffs, and by the adoption of a common uniform policy towards foreigners, strive to attain to the same degree of commercial and industrial development to which other nations have attained by means of their commercial policy. . . .

The German nation cannot be complete so long as it does not

15 extend over the whole coast, from the mouth of the Rhine to the frontier of Poland, including *Holland* and *Denmark*. A natural consequence of this union must be the admission of both these countries into the German *Bund*, and consequently into the German nationality. . . . Besides, both these nations belong, as

20 respects their descent and whole character, to the German nationality. . . .

The history of the trade and industry of North America is more instructive for our subject than any other can be. . . . Americans came to realise the truth that it behoves a great nation not to set its

25 heart exclusively upon the enjoyment of proximate material advantages; that civil power, a more important and desirable possession than mere material wealth, as Adam Smith himself allows – can be secured and retained only by the creation of a manufacturing power of its own. . . .

> Excerpts from Friedrich List (1925) *The National System of Political Economy (1789–1846)* (Stuttgart) quoted in L. L. Snyder *op. cit.*

30 (ii) No doubt this great Union which is known in Germany by the name of *Zollverein* . . . derived its first and strongest influence from a desire to get rid of those barriers to intercommunication which the separate fiscal legislation of the various states of Germany raised among a people whom natural and national feelings, as well as
35 common interests, would otherwise have connected more intimately and permanently together. . . .

The Commercial League [i.e. the *Zollverein*] is, in fact, the substantial representative of a sentiment widely, if not universally, spread in Germany – that of national unity. It has done wonders in
40 breaking down petty and local prejudices, and has become a foundation on which future legislation, representing the common interests of the German people, may undoubtedly be hereafter raised. If well directed in its future operation, the *Zollverein* will represent the fusion of German interests in one great alliance . . . the
45 League has been [so] much strengthened by the experience of its benefits – that its popularity is extending . . . [and] its further spreading may be confidently anticipated.

In fact the *Zollverein* has brought the sentiment of German nationality out of the regions of hope and fancy into those of
50 positive and material interests . . . it may become . . . an instrument not only for promoting the peace and prosperity of the states that compose it, but of extending their friendly relations throughout the world. . . .

> John Bowring *Report on the Prussian Commercial Union*, *British Parliamentary Papers* (16 January–August 1840), vol VI, pp 381–388

(iii) The Germany Confederation cannot be considered a really effective political institution . . . unless it remains completely
55 faithful to the principle of equality of rights and duties among the members of the federal body. Special privileges for any powers whatsoever are banned by the Confederation . . . (with the exception that the Presidency of the *Diet* is officially recognised as belonging to Austria). . . .
60 The situation has changed as a result of the formation of the Prussian Customs Union. Now a number of independent states accept, in relation to a neighbour superior in power, the obligation of conforming to *its* laws. . . .

Within the great Confederation, a smaller confederation is being
65 formed ... under the direction of Prussia and by the necessary
formation of common interests, the states which make up this
union will compose a more or less compact body. ... Under such
circumstances, there can be no more useful discussions in the *Diet*.
Such debates will be replaced by votes agreed upon in advance and
70 motivated, not by the interests of the Confederation, but by the
exclusive rights of Prussia. ...

Prussia ... will use the satisfaction of material interests to
weaken the influence of Austria over the courts dedicated to her
system, to sabotage their relations with Austria, to make them used
75 to the idea of turning their eyes to Berlin. ...

> Metternich to the Emperor, June 1833, quoted in Prince
> Clemens Metternich (1882) *Mémoires* (Paris) vol V pp 524,
> 528

Questions

a What does the author mean by a nation's 'own individual
powers' (line 9)? What would be the 'common uniform policy
towards foreigners' (lines 10–11)?

★ b What was the plausibility of Holland and Denmark joining the
German Bund at this time?

c Explain the author's intention in his discussion of North America in the last paragraph of the first passage.

d Does the author of the second passage see the motivating force
behind the foundation of the *Zollverein* as primarily political or
economic?

★ e What 'wonders' had the *Zollverein* done in 'breaking down petty
and local prejudices' (line 40)?

f Is the author of the second passage rational in his assessment of
the role of the *Zollverein*?

g Comment on Metternich's perception of 'the principle of equality of rights and duties among members of the federal body'
(lines 55–56).

★ h Which were the 'independent states' (line 6) now members of
the *Zollverein*?

i What is to be understood by 'the necessary formation of
common interests' (lines 65–66)?

★ j Were Metternich's predictions alarmist rather than accurate?

5 A clarion call for Liberal nationalism

Germany, great, prosperous, mighty Germany, should have taken
the front rank in the society of European states, but, plundered by
traitorous families of aristocrats, she has been erased from the list of

European states and is scorned by foreign peoples. Destined by
nature to become the guardian in Europe of enlightenment, freedom and international order, German power has been turned
upside down to the suppression of freedom of all peoples. . . .
    . . . the reform of Germany, as the basis for the reorganisation of
Europe, is a great, common concern for all the peoples of our area
of the world. Upon it depends the welfare of the great majority of
all the nations of Europe. . . . Even France can never attain
freedom, happiness and peace for any length of time unless there be
a liberation and rejuvenation of Germany, because the incompatible
principles of people's sovereignty and divine right monarchy
engender eternal friction and must kindle wars. This can be
resolved only by the decisive triumph of the rational principle, that
is, the triumph of the people's sovereignty in Germany. . . . But we
can expect little or no help from France in our struggle for the
Fatherland. We do not wish to buy our freedom at the price of
another disgrace: namely, the relinquishing of the left bank of the
Rhine to France. . . .
    When the purest, most capable, and most courageous patriots
have agreed upon suitable measures for the reform of our country
and also have joined together and published journals to win public
opinion of all the people for these reforms, even though they be
only 20 men filled with national pride, civic dignity, and the flame
of love for freedom . . . then will the strength of traitors be
consumed into the dust. . . .
    Therefore, German patriots, we shall elect men, who have been
predestined because of their spirit, fiery zeal and character, to begin
and lead the great work of German reform. . . . May this magnificent alliance then become the destiny of our people. . . . Three
cheers for the unified, free states of Germany! Hail! Three cheers
for federated, republican Europe!

> Extract from a speech by Johann Wirth at Hambach
> National Festival, 27 May 1832, taken from *Das National-
> fest der Deutschen zu Hambach* (Neustadt on Haardt, 1832)
> *passim*

Questions

  a Explain the significance of the claim that Germany was 'plun-
      dered by traitorous families of aristocrats' (lines 2–3).
★ *b* How and why was Germany 'scorned by foreign peoples'
      (line 4)?
  c What was 'the suppression of freedom of all peoples' (line 7)?
  d The passage may be considered a curious fusion of shrewd
      analysis and hot rhetoric. Give examples of *both*.
  e Comment on the author's anxieties concerning 'the left bank of
      the Rhine' (lines 20–21).

6 Frederick William IV appeals to his 'Beloved Berliners', 19 March 1848

The shout of joy which greeted me from innumerable faithful hearts still resounded in my ears when a crowd of peace-breakers mingled with the loyal throng, making seditious and bold demands, and augmenting in numbers as the bold withdrew. As their
5 impetuous intrusion extended to the very portals of the Palace ... the courtyard was cleared by the cavalry, at *walking pace and their weapons sheathed*; and two guns of the infantry went off of themselves, without, thanks be to God! causing any injury. A band of wicked men, chiefly consisting of foreigners who, although
10 searched for, have succeeded in concealing themselves for more than a week ... and have filled the excited minds of my faithful and beloved Berliners with thoughts of vengeance for supposed bloodshed; and thus have they become fearful authors of bloodshed themselves.

My troops, your brothers and fellow countrymen, did not make
15 use of their weapons till forced to do so by several shots fired at them from the Königstrasse. The victorious advance of the troops was the necessary consequence.

It is now yours, inhabitants of my beloved native city, to avert a fearful evil. .... Remove the barricades which are still standing ... I
20 pledge you my royal truth that all the streets and squares shall be instantaneously cleared of the troops, and the military garrisons shall be confined solely to the most important buildings. ...

Forget the past, as I shall forget it, for the sake of the great future which, under the peace-giving blessing of God, is dawning upon
25 Prussia and through Prussia upon all Germany. ...

> Extract from *Annual Register* ed. M. Epstein (1848) (London, 1761 *et seq.*) pp 378–379

Questions

★ *a* Who were the 'peace-breakers' (line 2) in the episode described by Frederick William?

★ *b* Discuss the circumstances which led up to the issue of this proclamation.

c How correct was the King's apportionment of blame to those 'wicked men' who had 'filled the excited minds of my faithful and beloved Berliners' (lines 9–12)?

d How noteworthy were the concessions offered by the King in this extract? Is his tone conciliatory or abject?

7 The *Vorparlament* experiment

(i) The power of extraordinary events, the demands which have been expressed loudly throughout our fatherland, and the past calls of the state governments have led, in this great hour, to this great Assembly, such as has never been seen in our history.

5   The best of our old political life is revealed in the basic principles of this Assembly, which has been greeted with joy and confidence by the entire German people. It is a great new achievement – the German parliament.

    The German governments and their common body, the *Bund*,
10 are united with the German people in their similar love for our great fatherland. We greet with joy the spirit of the times, and extend our hand of welcome to the national representatives and wish them good luck and good fortune.

> Opening of the German National Assembly, 18 May 1848 in Frankfurt, Message from the *Bund*, taken from Max Schilling (1848) *Quellenbuch zur Geschichte der Neuzeit* (Berlin) p 421

(ii) We must ourselves create the provisional central authority . . .
15 the future central authority must be placed in the hands of a regent with responsible ministers.

    It is necessary that we choose a regent from the highest sphere, for in circumstances that exist now there is no private person, as perhaps some individuals, or even parties, have thought, who
20 could assume the office.

    . . . there will be found in my proposal no surrender of the principle [of the nation's sovereignty], even if my opinion should be, as indeed it is, that this exalted personage must be a prince, which you must concede, not because of, but despite, the fact that
25 he is a prince.

    . . . many bitter things have just been said of our princes, and the love of mankind has always been dear to me. But . . . to bear hatred against whole generations . . . is not magnanimous.

    Let us unite as far as union is possible! Let us sacrifice what must
30 be sacrificed in order to obtain and to lighten the passage toward better conditions. We do not compromise liberty, and we consti-tute the unity of our nation and Fatherland, for which we have yearned so long.

> Henrich von Gagern to the Frankfurt National Assembly, in an extract from the *Stenographischer Bericht* of the occa-sion, edited by Franz Wigard (Leipzig, 1848) vol I, p 114

Questions

a How true was it that 'demands . . . have been expressed loudly throughout our Fatherland' (lines 1–2)?

b Comment on the claim that the German governments and the *Bund* were 'united with the German people in their similar love for our great Fatherland' (lines 9–11).

d   Why did the 'circumstances that exist now' make it impossible
for a 'private person' to become regent (line 18)?
e   What does the author mean in claiming that 'the love of
mankind has always been dear to me' (lines 26–27)?
★   f   'Let us sacrifice what must be sacrificed ...' (lines 29–30).
Comment on the unfolding of events which resulted in this
statement.

8   The King of Prussia refuses the Crown of Germany

(i) Gentlemen, the message which you have come to give me has
deeply moved me. It has turned my eyes to the king of kings. ...
This call which you make upon me gives me a title which I know
how to prize. It demands incalculable sacrifices from me if I accept
5   it. ... The German National Assembly has counted on me for
everything which is required for the establishment of the unity and
strength of Germany. ... I am ready to prove by my actions that
their reliance on my fidelity, my love and my devotion to the cause
of my country has not been misplaced. But, gentlemen, I should
10   not justify that confidence – I should not answer the expectations of
the German people, I should not be upholding the cause of German
unity – if I violated sacred rights and broke the explicit and solemn
promises I had given before, by omitting to gain the voluntary
assent of the crowned heads, princes and free states of Germany,
15   before taking a resolution that is bound to have such decisive
consequences for them and for the German people they rule over.
. . .

> The King's reply to a deputation from the Frankfurt
> Parliament, 4 April 1849. Extract from *Select Documents in
> European History* vol III, (Methuen, 1931) pp 129–130

(ii) Using the pretence that they are working in the interests of
Germany, the enemies of the fatherland have raised high the
20   standard of revolt, first in neighbouring Saxony, and then in
several districts of south Germany. To my utter dismay, even in
sections of our own land, some have allowed themselves to be
seduced into following this standard and attempting, in open
rebellion, against the constituted government, to overturn the
25   order established by both divine and human sanction. ...
I was not able to submit a favourable reply to the offer of a crown
by the German National Assembly because that body does not have
the right, without the consent of the German governments, to
bestow the crown they have offered me, and because, in addition,
30   they tendered the crown upon the condition that I would accept a

constitution which could not be reconciled with the rights and safety of the German states.

I have tried in every possible way to reach an understanding with the German National Assembly. Now it has broken with Prussia. The majority of its members are no longer those upon whom Germany looked with pride and confidence. Most of the deputies voluntarily left the Assembly when it became obvious that it was on the road to ruin. Yesterday, I myself ordered all the Prussian deputies who had not already left, to be recalled. The other governments will do the same.

A party now dominating the Assembly is in league with the terrorists. While they urge the unity of Germany as a pretence, they are really fighting the battle of godlessness, perjury, and theft, and arousing a war. . . .

> Frederick William IV's 'To My People!' at Charlottenburg, 15 May 1849, quoted in L. L. Snyder (1958) *Documents of German History* (Rutgers) pp 186–187

Questions

a What were the 'incalculable sacrifices' demanded of the king (line 4)?

b Comment on the 'sacred rights' and 'solemn promises' alluded to in lines 12–13.

c What is the general tenor of the first passage? In what respects, despite the identical authorship, is the second remarkably different?

d Whom *precisely* did the king mean by 'the enemies of the fatherland' (line 19)?

e Consider the different reasons given by the king both for his reluctance and his refusal to accept the crown. Which in the end do you consider to have been decisive?

f What did the king understand by 'the rights and safety of the German states' (lines 31–32)? How may this have been different from the founders of the *Vorparlament*?

★ g Explain how it was that the German National Assembly had 'broken with Prussia' (line 34)?

★ h How receptive was the Prussian audience likely to have been to the words of the king in the second passage?

II Reversing the Legacy of 1848

The historian William Carr has commented that 'the tragedy of the German Revolution [of 1848] must be seen against the European background of which it was an integral part'. However, much of that failure was bound up with the inability of the liberals in the Frankfurt Assembly to achieve a consensus, either on the right or left of the Chamber. This was shown most clearly by the refusal of King Frederick William of Prussia to accept the German Crown. Their collapse delighted Bismarck, an extremely outspoken and illiberal figure who had tried to persuade the king to launch a *coup d'état*. It augured badly, however, for the future of the Frankfurt Assembly and, also perhaps, for the future of liberal thought within Germany as a whole.

As the detritus of the 1848 Revolution apparently dispelled itself, more traditional rivalries re-emerged. These reached a flashpoint over Prussia's founding of the Erfurt Union which, had she had her own way, would have allowed her to dominate a federal state excluding Austria from Germany effectively, but which would have drawn authority from a loose association of states based on a common foreign and commercial policy. This, at least, had been the plan of General Josef von Radowitz, a close friend of the King of Prussia who in May 1849 took advantage of Austria's distraction in Hungary and Italy to obtain the agreement of 130 members of the former Frankfurt Parliament to pursue this idea. The Austrian Minister President, Felix zu Schwarzenburg, was appalled at this prospect but, until free of fighting, sought to buy time by signing the Interim with Prussia, whereby the two nations agreed to administer Germany jointly until May 1850.

But, once Austria could again concentrate on German affairs, events turned sharply in her favour. Schwarzenburg helped to manipulate the secession of Saxony and Hanover away from the League of Three Kings, formed by Radowitz the previous year. They had hitherto felt themselves with little option but to go along with Prussian plans. Moreover, in the war between Denmark and Germany which had broken out in 1849 over the duchies of Schleswig and Holstein, Russia now put strong pressure on Prussia to make a generous peace. The final peace settlement even allowed for Confederate troops to restore order in Holstein. This held out the alarming prospect of Austrian troops marching into that area adjacent to Prussia about which she was most acutely sensitive. To this was added further provocation: in response to an appeal from the Elector of Hesse-Cassel who was facing a collapse of civil order, Austrian troops marched north, crossing the vital strategic roads linking the Rhineland and Brandenburg.

Yet even now Prussia hesitated. Radowitz, having failed to persuade the Council of Ministers to mobilise, resigned. The king, after a brief skirmish, accepted the occupation of Hesse-Cassel by federal troops. This agreement was signed by the new foreign minister, Otto von Manteuffel at Olmutz and marked the abandonment of the Erfurt Union.

Schwarzenburg, for Austria, had won a notable victory but its legacy was not straightforward. Prussia continued fiercely to oppose plans to incorporate the Habsburg Empire into the German Confederation, and in this she could count on considerable support from France and Britain, and even from Russia. Although Frederick William prompted the signing of a three-year alliance between Prussia and Austria in 1851, this was done more to appease conservative opinion at home than to tackle areas of major dissent. Austria was still no nearer securing the reform of the Confederation that she sought. Prussia still failed to obtain a statutory recognition of the parity of status she claimed for herself alongside Austria within the Confederation.

It is in this context that the first skirmishes over the *Zollverein* are best understood. Schwarzenburg died in 1852, but his successor in the Ministry of Commerce, Rudolph von Bruck, sought to build a huge central European Customs Union from the Black Sea to the Baltic. Prussia, jealous of her own economic ascendancy in north and central Germany, predictably opposed such a scheme. The economic allegiances of the southern German states thus became of paramount importance and, not unreasonably, most of these states sought to delay undertaking a firm commitment to one side or the other. Delbrück, an official in the Prussian Ministry of Commerce, persuaded Hanover and Oldenburg to join the *Zollverein* by 1851. The remaining southern states were in the main agreed by 1853 that their economic welfare was too closely bound up with the *Zollverein* to leave it lightly and in 1853, the Customs Union was renewed for another 12 years. This marked a most significant political victory for Prussia and, arguably, it is from this time on that Austrian policy became a fundamentally defensive one.

1 The Revolutionary Legacy of 1848: two responses

(a) When the king declined the imperial crown on April 3 1849, but drew from the decree of the Frankfurt Assembly a 'title' of whose

value he was well aware, he was principally moved to do this because of the revolutionary, or at any rate, parliamentary source
5 of the offer. . . .

When I note the conditions both personal and material in the Prussia of those days as not ripe for the assumption of the leadership of Germany in war and peace, I do not mean to say that I then foresaw it with the same clearness as I see it today. . . . My
10 satisfaction in those days at the refusal of the imperial crown by the king was due, not to the judgement I had formed of his personal qualities, but rather to a keener sensitiveness for the prestige of the Prussian crown and its wearer, and still more to my instinctive distrust of the developments of events since the barricades of 1848
15 and their parliamentary consequences. As regards the latter, I and my political friends were under the impression that the leading men in parliament and in the press . . . promoted and carried out the programme of 'making a clean sweep of everything' and that the actual ministers were not the men to direct or check such a
20 movement. . . .

A speedy utilisation of the situation in a national sense was possible, perhaps, but presupposed clear and practical aims and resolute action. Both were wanting. The favourable time was lost in considering the details of the future constitution. . . .

The Memoirs of Otto von Bismarck vol I (New York, 1899) pp 63–65

25 (b) The signatories below are convinced that this constitution was the only formula available in the given circumstances, for a peaceful solution and a reconciliation of the interests and rights of the various German races, states and dynasties. . . . Guided by this conviction, the signatories have so far co-operated in all the
30 decisions, which by the appropriate constitutional means and through public opinion could have brought each individual state to recognise the constitution of the *Reich*. . . . To their deep grief events have assumed a different complexion and the hopes of the German nation, so near fulfilment, seem likely to miscarry. . . .
35 [Though] faced by the very great dangers threatening the Fatherland, four German kings, including the Prussian king himself, have declined the formula of mediation between the conflicting principles threatening our times which the *Reich* constitution offered. . . . Finally, since 10 May, a series of decisions has been taken by a
40 new majority in the Assembly, which are, in part, impossible to execute and, in part, quite contradictory to the course pursued by the earlier majority to which the signatories belonged. In this position of affairs, the National Assembly has only one choice, *either*, by setting aside what has so far been the Central Power, to
45 tear asunder the last common, legal bond between all German governments and peoples, and to foment a civil war, *or* to renounce

the execution of the *Reich* constitution by means of an act of legislation and to do so in co-operation with the provisional Central Power. The signatories have considered the second of these two evils the lesser for the Fatherland. . . .

> Declaration of Dahlmann and 65 others when leaving the National Assembly, 21 May 1849, in P. Wentzcke (1922) *Die erste deutsche Nationalversammlung und ihr Werk* (Munich)

Questions

a Explain Bismarck's reference to the 'revolutionary, or at any rate, parliamentary source of the offer' (lines 4–5).

b Comment on what Bismarck understood by 'conditions both personal and material in the Prussia of those days' (lines 6–7).

c What did Bismarck's 'keener sensitiveness for the prestige of the Prussian Crown' (lines 12–13) lead him to conclude about developments in 1848?

d How influential were Bismarck and his 'political friends' (line 16) at this time?

e What is the justice of Bismarck's claim that 'clear and practical aims and resolute action . . . [were] . . . wanting' (lines 22–23)?

f Explain the reference to the 'events' having assumed 'a different complexion' (line 33).

g What were the 'very great dangers threatening the Fatherland' (lines 35–36)?

h Why were the decisions taken since 10 May (line 39) so objectionable to the signatories of this Declaration?

i How realistic were the hopes espoused by those who framed this Declaration?

2 An early sparring match over the future of the Zollverein

He [Bruck of Austria]: Allusion to the political complications between Austria and Prussia. Assurance that it would be recognised that it was in the interests of Austria that Prussia should be powerful and strong against revolution from within and storms from without. One will come to terms with Prussia politically eventually, but time presses and the economic union must be pushed forward, in order to reach political union. . . . He was delighted that Prussia had shown herself acquiescent; the question of form was not within his competence.

10   *I [Delbrück of Prussia]:* The question of form included matters of
        substance. . . .
            He: In Austria we must insist that the Customs Union should be
        established immediately by treaty. That was said in the memo-
        randum.
15   *I:* But the memorandum had a new treaty in view.
            He: Yes, but new only in its detail . . . .
            I: But they were the essential things . . . .
                Note by Delbrück, 6 March 1850 (Merseburg, Deutsches
                Zentralarchiv, Rep. 92. Nachlass Delbrück, vol II, p 6),
                quoted in H. Böhme (1971) *The Foundation of the German
                Empire* (Oxford University Press)

Questions

a Comment on Bruck's assertion that 'economic union must be
     pushed forward in order to reach political union' (lines 6–7).
b What is Delbrück essentially seeking to do in this extract?
c To what extent does this extract shed light on the dilemma faced
     by the King of Württemberg discussed in Document 2?

3 The Convention of Olmütz

1. The Governments of Austria and Prussia declare that it is their
intention by means of a decision of all the German governments, to
procure the final and definitive regulation of the Hessian and
Holstein questions . . . .
5   3. But since it is a matter of common interest that in Holstein, as
well as in Hesse, a legal state, and one congenial to the federal
duties, may be quickly introduced, and since, moreover, Austria,
for herself and her allies, has to the full given her guarantees
required by Prussia, which protect her interests in the occupation of
10 Electoral Hesse, these two governments of Austria and Prussia
have agreed on the following . . . :
(a) in Electoral Hesse, Prussia will place nothing in the way of the
troops which the Elector has called in. For this purpose she will
instruct her generals to consent to the federal troops crossing the
15 Etappe roads, which are now occupied by Prussia. The two
governments of Austria and their allies will ask His Royal Highness's the Elector's consent to the presence in Cassel of one
batallion of the troops, who have marched in at the desire of His
Royal Highness, and of one batallion of Prussia's troops, for the
20 better preservation of order and tranquillity.
(b) Austria and Prussia, after previously conferring with their
allies, at the earliest convenience, will send commissioners to
Holstein, who, in the name of the Confederation, shall desire the

Stadholders to suspend hostilities ... and to reduce their army to
25   one third of its present strength. ...
Olmutz, November 29, 1850.   SCHWARZENBURG
                                                             MANTEUFFEL
        Text of the Convention of Olmutz, November 1850,
        quoted in L. L. Snyder (1958) *Documents of German History*
        (Rutgers University Press) pp 195–196

Questions

a   Discuss the precise political circumstances which resulted in the
       publication of this 'joint' declaration.
b   Was it a matter of common interest that 'a legal state and one
       congenial to the federal duties' be created in Holstein (lines 5–
       6)?
c   Why might the beginning of Clause 3(a) be considered the most
       critical clause in the entire Convention?
d   How far did the Convention of Olmutz remove the grievances
       it sought to remedy?

4   Bismarck as an early champion of Prussian interests

(a) The only healthy foundation for a large state – and this is what
distinguishes it from a small state – is state egoism rather than
romanticism, and it is unworthy of a great state to fight for
something which does not affect its own interest. Gentlemen, show
5   me an objective worth a war and I will go along with you. It is easy
enough for a statesman to ride the popular wave from the comfort
of his own fireside, making thunderous speeches from the rostrum,
letting the public sound the trumpets of war, and leaving it to the
musketeer, bleeding out his life's blood in the snowy wastes, to
10   settle whether policies end in glory or in failure. Nothing is simpler
– but woe to any statesman who, at such a time, fails to find a cause
of war which will stand up to scrutiny once the fighting is over.
        Bismarck's speech to Parliament, Erfurt, 3 December
        1850, quoted in H. Böhme *op. cit.*

(b) Very well, said Bismarck in effect, if he could not extract
Austria's acknowledgement of Prussian equality, at least he had a
15   powerful nuisance value and could make it very difficult for Vienna
to get her way in all sorts of matters. In his own vivid phrase:
'When Austria hitches a horse in front, we hitch one behind.'
Travelling laboriously from court to court in southern Germany,
he worked to influence the rulers and their ministers over the heads
20   of their representatives at Frankfurt, cajoling, flattering, bribing,

playing one against the other, sowing distrust of Austria, sometimes threatening.

Too much has been made of the personal hostility Bismarck felt
towards Count von Thun. This existed, of course. From the start
25 he felt himself slighted by the aristocrat who, as he saw it,
concealed the morals of a card-sharper behind an air of false
amiability. He may well have felt some jealousy of a dazzling
magnate who came of a family rich beyond the dreams of any
Junker and represented a culture no less superior. ... The count,
30 moreover, was a master of that casual, offhand, gratuitous offen-
siveness, as much a mark of Austrian officialdom as was its
unreliability and idleness. ... Bismarck was never casual, and he
never broke a promise by accident or out of slackness. He did not
cheat unconsciously, and he held in especial contempt those who
35 cheated without clearly realising what they were doing. With his
downright aspect he brought a note of foreboding into his relations
with the Austrian representative.

Fifteen years later it was to end in armed conflict; but not for a
long time did Bismarck begin to feel that war between Prussia and
40 Austria was inevitable. Inevitability was a concept he instinctively
rejected: the lives of nations as well as of individuals were so full of
accidents. His understanding of this was an important element in
his genius. Equally certainly, even in his first brushes with the
Austrians he saw, looking far ahead, that war must be considered as
45 a possibility: the greatest service a statesman could do was to keep
his mind open to all possibilities.

Although he was certainly irritated by Austrian ways and
pretentions, he was also kicking against the constraints of official
protocol and the extreme tiresomeness of having to treat fools
50 gladly. His celebrated demonstrations against Count von Thun –
lighting a cigar at meetings where by custom the count was the
only man to smoke; pulling off his own jacket when the count held
court in shirt sleeves; refusing to wait when the count was not
ready to receive him at the time agreed – all these ... were protests
55 against fate at least as much as they were demonstrations against
Austria.
E. Crankshaw (1981) *Bismarck* (Macmillan) pp 70–71

Questions

a   Of what (and of whom) was Bismarck possibly thinking in his
    reference to a statesman riding 'the popular wave from the
    comfort of his own fireside' (lines 6–7)?
b   Does the first passage have a moral standpoint? If so, is it an
    unconventional one?
c   What is meant by the 'Austrian acknowledgement of Prussian
    equality' (line 14)?

d   Why does the author suggest that too much may be made of the hostility between Bismarck and Thun (lines 23–25)?

e   Comment upon the positive aspects of Bismarck's character suggested in this passage.

f   Why had 'Austrian ways and pretensions' (lines 47–48) been allowed to hold sway until this time?

g   How may Document 3 and both Documents 4(a) and 4(b) each influence any understanding of each other and qualify any assumptions we might otherwise make?

5   The start of economic warfare: a medium-sized state finds itself torn between Austria and Prussia

(a) Guided by the strongest wish that the negotiations to be opened on the subject [of a Customs Union] may lead, through the sincere co-operation of all the state governments, to a firm and lasting union embracing the whole of Germany, the government here will
5   most readily accept the prospective invitation to take part in a meeting to be instituted to that end and, in association with other governments participating in the *Zollverein*, it will make the furthering of that purpose the object of its most eager endeavour.

    This government believes that it may indulge the hope that it
10   will be able to derive the utmost profit from the harmonising of the commercial policy (of which it has always been the spokesman in the *Zollverein*) with the principles indicated by the Imperial Austrian ministry as its guidelines for the revision of the customs tariff.

> E. Wächter or Württemberg Foreign Office to Handel, Austrian envoy in Stuttgart, 6 March 1850, (Vienna, Haus-Hof-und Stattsarchiv, PA II, no. 75)

15   (b) We have now reached a point where the alternatives are self-evident: whether it is advisable for Württemberg to renew the *Zollverein* with Prussia or to strive for a Customs Union with Austria.

    In our judgement there is no third course . . . each of the two
20   chief Powers, on account of its particular economic and financial interests, is going to exert itself to obstruct and weaken the other's influence over the rest of the *Zollverein* states and, indeed, to seek to force it entirely out . . . nothing remains for the other states except to take a stand likewise upon their own interests and to take their
25   decisions straight from this standpoint.

    In making her decision on this matter Württemberg will, similarly, take her own advantage into consideration. We, on our side, are not in doubt about the course to advise between these alternatives

... A breach of the tariff links with Prussia, who rules the Rhine for
30 a long stretch on both banks, would cause the most damaging
disturbance of trade. ... So ... during the 18 years that the
Zollverein has existed, contacts in trade have become so many and
the interests of the businessmen have so interlocked with each
other, that the tearing apart of these countries, which have econo-
35 mically grown together, would be accompanied by the most
damaging effects upon industry and trade and connected with
enormous losses of capital. No time could be more unsuited,
moreover, for such disturbances and losses to be sustained, than
just this present period, when the transition from small industry to
40 large-scale factory manufacture is being completed and when, for
that very reason, so many handicraftsmen are readily inclined to
ascribe blame to the governments for the consequences of natural
economic development ...

The removal of the Austrian tariff barrier in a year or two would
45 offer no adequate compensation for all this dislocation ...
Württemberg and Baden do not come in the first rank in relation to
Austria, partly because they are too far from the centre of the
Austrian state, ... and partly because countries such as, for
example, Saxony, which are industrially more advanced, would
50 quite definitely get in first. ...

Moreover, ... an active trade of some significance has sprung up
quite recently between the south German states, particularly
Württemberg, and north Germany, particularly Prussia ...

There is to be added a consideration of commercial politics. ...
55 Were Austria to enter the *Zollverein*, with her population
of 38 000 000 (not counting Modena and Parma) she would be
stronger than Prussia and the other German states taken together,
and more than twice as strong as the states taken without Prussia.
... It could easily, therefore, happen that those states which broke
60 away from Prussia and attached themselves to Austria would sink
in matters of commercial policy to an appendage of that great state.
... It is different in relation to Prussia. The medium-sized and
small states of Germany ... have a population of only 15 000 000
therefore half a million less than that of the whole Prussian state.
65 [This] will guarantee them a stronger influence on the conduct and
the course of the *Zollverein*'s affairs ...

> Report of the Württemberg Central Office for Industry
> and Trade to the Württemberg Ministry of Finance, 17
> December 1851, (Stuttgart, Württembergisches Haupt-
> staatsarchiv, E.222, Fach. 193, no. 1164)

(c) His Majesty [the King of Württemberg] of course wishes for
the Austro-German Customs and Trade Union, but has not yet
been able to convince himself that it is *inevitable*, if only our allies
70 hold firm; because Prussia, without endangering to the utmost her

financial and political interests, *cannot* give up the *Zollverein* and the bond with south Germany.

Because then the king is not thoroughly convinced of this, and because from financial considerations, he is continually anxious lest
75 he bring the *Zollverein* into danger through too definite pronounce- ments, he is hesitant and slow to follow the way we have indicated to him. . . .

> Handel (Austrian envoy in Stuttgart) to Buol, 15 May 1852, (Vienna, Haus-Hof-und Staatsarchiv, PA II, no. 78)

Questions

a What is the tone adopted by the writer in Passage 5(a)?
b What do you understand by the 'harmonising of commercial policy' (lines 10–11)?
c Comment upon the reasons given in this report as to why 'Württemberg will, similarly, take her own advantage into consideration' (lines 26–27). What was her 'advantage'?
d Explain the references to 'this present period, when the transi- tion from small industry to large-scale factory manufacture is being completed' (lines 39–40).
e Explain the reference to Modena and Parma in line 56.
f Was it correct for the writer to claim (lines 59–61) that there was 'no third course' or have the choices been deliberately painted in very stark terms?
g How much weight do you believe the considerations of 'com- mercial politics' (line 54) carried with the decision makers compared to the evidence given earlier in the passage?
h Does Passage 5(a) probably represent an honest statement of intention? Does Passage 5(c) mark a complete turnabout in thinking? How far does Passage 5(b) go towards explaining such a turnabout?

6   Austrophobia?

(a) Prussia was able to give up the Erfurt Union and return to the Federal *Diet*, because the Confederation of 1815 is simply an international league in which a state of Prussia's power and standing may hope to be able to assert its independence even
5 against a majority of smaller states. Prussia, however, can never comply with the Austrian demands in commercial policy without denying the whole political position she has up to now held. . . . Prussia must therefore make it her resolve in commercial policy to maintain the *Zollverein*'s power of free self-determination, which is
10 independent of any Austrian veto. However painful she may find a separation from the Confederation of 1815 and the disturbance of

the long-accustomed relationships in many parts of the country and branches of industry, even so in this question of political life or death, Prussia will be obliged, quite decisively, to prefer a north German but independent *Zollverein* to a greater Customs Union dependent upon Austria.

15

Extract from the *Constitutionelle Zeitung*, 9 April 1852

(b) The Austrians invariably cheat at cards and always will. With their measureless ambition I do not see how we can expect ever to make an honest alliance with them.

Bismarck to Kleist-Retzow, 4 July 1851, quoted in E. Crankshaw (1981) *Bismarck* (Macmillan) p 74

Questions

a   What was the Erfurt Union (line 1)?
b   When and why did Prussia leave it to return to the German Confederation?
c   Discussion the fairness of calling the Confederation 'simply an international league' (lines 2–3).
d   What were the demands Austria was making in commercial policy? Were they as threatening to Prussia's political position as suggested here (line 7)?
e   What evidence is there for suggesting that at this time Prussia would have found a separation from the German Confederation 'painful' (line 10).
f   Are these reports too partisan to be effective? Whose views in Prussia do you imagine they did *not* encompass?

III War and Opportunism, 1854–1861

The outbreak of the Crimean War in 1854 marked the onset of a change in the relationship of Germany, and Austria most especially, with the other Great Powers of Europe. Moreover, it created serious strains within the Confederation. Bismarck, still the Prussian representative on the Confederation *Diet*, urged his government to exploit the chill between Russia and Austria, which grew out of Austria's benevolent neutrality to Britain and France during the Crimean hostilities. The Government still tended to distrust (and to some extent discount) Bismarck, but with the coming of peace in 1856 and the signing of the Treaty of Paris, it was evident that Russia was no longer in any position to maintain the Vienna Settlement.

Bismarck, desperate that the fluidity of this situation should not be squandered, argued that Prussia now held the pivotal position between a revisionist France and Russia on the one hand, and between Britain and Austria, keen to maintain the *status quo* on the other. It was in March 1858 that he urged, openly, the radical step of harnessing the movement for German nationalism as a means of destroying Austria's influence in Germany. This vision of *kleindeutschland* (a small Germany – that is, one without Austria) was received cautiously in Berlin. Prince William, who became regent that year, personally was wary of Bismarck and sent him as ambassador, first to St Petersburg and then to Paris. A stream of radical memoranda poured out from both places, far-sighted and cynical, but not as yet acted upon.

Arguably, the two mobilising factors were, firstly, the arrival of the regent and, secondly, the outbreak of war between Austria and France in 1859. Prince William was a sober, deeply conservative figure, but one deeply resentful of Prussian humiliation at Olmutz and the repository of Liberal hopes in the 1850s. He dismissed the Manteuffel ministry and set about a cautious programme of domestic reform. This suited most Liberals admirably: content with the 1850 Constitution, they had no desire whatever for universal suffrage which they believed would mean their having to contend with conservative, rather than radical, predilections of the masses.

However, the French successes in their war against the Austrians in 1859, and the (as yet incomplete) achievement of Italian self-realisation which followed in 1860 saw a resurgence of German nationalism. The especial fear was that Napoleon III, who clearly had designs on the Rhine, had come to an understanding with Russia giving him a free hand at such a time when the Austrians were defeated. A wave of Francophobia seized Prussia. The regent was more equivocal: he held out to Austria the prospect of military assistance if Prussia could be given sole control of the federal forces in the event of an attack from the west. Austria, fearful of surrendering her hegemony in north Germany, refused. She was in turn defeated by France and lost Lombardy in consequence by the terms of the Peace of Villfranca. Prussia faced bitter vilification in Germany as a whole for her inactivity to her neighbour in distress.

But, within Prussia, the events of 1859 exposed the military weakness and need for radical reform within the Confederation. This prompted a movement calling for a strong central authority emanating from Prussia itself. That August, leading Liberals met at Eisenach, hammering out a programme for a national party committed to a Prussian-dominated unification. The *Nationalverein* saw the cementation of an alliance between Radicals and Liberals, united in a great national cause. William Carr has called it 'A pressure group more than a party' and it never had more than 25,000 members. Its value was to mobilise public opinion, but it had to be careful somehow to avoid alienating the support of southern states. Its catchment was heterogeneous: radicals and liberals were joined by financiers and industrialists, drawn by the brisk pragmatism of the Party who stressed the priority of power over principle. This early sighting of German *realpolitik* is a telling illustration of how far German Liberals had travelled since the heady days of 1848.

Thus, events conspired between 1859 and 1861 to see Liberals and Democrats working together enthusiastically in pursuit of a national ideal. Opposition was voiced most strongly by the Prussian landed nobility, fearful of an assault on their social and economic privileges in the event of unification. Likewise, their counterparts in other states, and especially in Bavaria, resented Prussia's arrogation of her own role deeply. Militarily and economically, however, there was little they could do. For that matter, Prussia had as yet come no nearer resolving any immediate plan of action to implement her aims and was anyway uncomfortably aware that, as her mobilisation of 1859 proved, her own army was sadly deficient. It was against this background that the regent sought in 1861 to undertake major Army reforms. Although not apparent until 1862, it was this particular issue which was to drive the precarious coalition of Crown and Liberals utterly apart.

1 The incompatibility of Austrian and Prussian policies in Germany

Vienna's policy has made Germany suddenly too small for us both. So long as an honourable arrangement over the influence of each in Germany is not reached and executed, we shall both plough the same narrow furrow, and ... Austria will remain the only state to
5 whom we continually lose and from whom we *could* continually gain. ... We have a great number of conflicting interests, which neither of us can give up, without renouncing the mission in which each believes for itself; they are, therefore, conflicts which cannot be peacefully unravelled by diplomatic correspondence. Even the
10 most serious pressure from abroad, the most urgent danger to the existence of us both, could not in 1813 nor in 1849 forge this iron. German dualism has for 1000 years ... settled our mutual relations by internal war. ... In this century, too, war alone will set the timepiece of history at its right hour.
15 I do not intend by this reasoning to reach the conclusion that we should immediately direct our policy by bringing about the *decision* between Austria and ourselves in as favourable circumstances as possible. I only wish to express my conviction that we shall be obliged, sooner or later, to fight Austria for our *existence* ... because
20 the course of events in Germany can have no other outcome. If this is correct ... then it is not possible for Prussia to take self denial to the point where she puts her own existence at stake in order to protect the integrity of Austria – in what is in my opinion a hopeless struggle. ...
Suppose we should be victorious against a Franco-Russian
25 alliance what in the end should we have fought for? For the maintenance of Austria's superiority in Germany and the pitiable constitution of the Germanic Confederation. We cannot possibly exert our last ounce of strength ... for that. Were we to seek, however, in co-operation with Austria to put through alterations to
30 the Germanic Confederation in our favour ... every deceit would be practised ... in order to prevent Prussia from reaching a higher standing within Germany. ...
If it came to the point when a Franco–Russian alliance with warlike purposes was an actuality, we should not, I think, join its
35 opponents because we should probably be defeated; we might be victorious, but we should have spent our blood *pour les beaux yeux de l'Autriche et de la Diète* ....

> Bismarck to Manteuffel, 26 April 1856, (O. von Bismarck *Gesammelte Werke*, vol ii, no. 152, p 138)

Questions

a What was it about Vienna's policy that had 'made Germany suddenly too small for us both' (line 1)?

   ★   *b*   Comment on the meaning of the phrase 'German dualism' (line 12).

   ★   *c*   What possible justification could Bismarck have for his observation that Prussia would 'be obliged, sooner or later, to fight Austria for our existence . . .' (lines 18–19)?

       d   What did Bismarck understand by Prussia taking 'self-denial to the point where she puts her own existence at stake' (lines 21–22)?

       e   Is the last paragraph of the extract a rational conclusion to the argument which precedes it or merely blind prejudice?

2   Bismarck reviews the relative threats posed by the Great Powers

(a) When I have been asked whether I was pro-Russian or pro-Western powers I have always answered: I am Prussian, and my ideal in foreign politics is total freedom from prejudice, independence of decision reached without pressure or aversion from or attraction to
5   other states and their rulers. I have had a certain sympathy for England and its inhabitants, and even now I am not altogether free of it; but they will not less us love them, and as far as I am concerned, as soon as it was proved to me that it was in the interests of a healthy and well considered Prussian policy I would see our
10 troops fire on French, English, or Austrians with equal satisfaction.

                Bismarck in a letter to Leopold von Gerlach, 11 May 1857,
                in *Gesammelte Werke* vol XIV, p 469

(b) For me, France, regardless of whoever stands at her head, is only one piece – though an essential one – in the chess game of politics. . . . I cannot as a Foreign Office official justify the harbouring of sympathies or antipathies towards foreign powers
15 either in myself or in others. Such a concept contains the embryo of disloyalty to the sovereign or the country. . . . In my view even the king himself has not the right to subordinate the interests of the fatherland to his feelings of love or hatred for foreigners. . . .

                Bismarck in a letter to Leopold von Gerlach, 2 May 1857,
                in *Gesammelte Werke* vol XIV, p 465

(c) The drive to conquest is no less present in England, North
20 America, Russia etc than in Napoleonic France; and as soon as might and opportunity present themselves moderation and justice do not easily set bounds, even for legitimate monarchs. But in Napoleon III this instinct does not seem to be dominant; he is no warlord . . . He will therefore turn to war only if he feels compelled
25 by *internal* necessity.

                Bismarck in a letter to Leopold von Gerlach, 30 May 1857,
                in *Gesammelte Werke* vol XIV, p 471

a Are the thoughts Bismarck outlined in lines 1–10 necessarily contradicted by the two extracts immediately after this and by his diatribe against Austria in extract 1 above?

★ b Comment on Bismarck's description of England which 'will not let us love them' (line 7).

c How fair is it to say that Bismarck was evidently determined not to overstate the risks Prussia faced from France at this time? If so, why was this?

d What inferences may one draw from the second of these extracts as to Bismarck's view of the relationship of the sovereign to the rest of the nation?

★ e Explain the reference to 'legitimate monarchs' (line 22).

3 Bruck argues for Austrian expansion

Austria should not stand solely on the defensive. She must go forward by acting decisively. She must advance along with German cultural life . . . accompanied and supported by the brisk rise of Austro–German commerce. Only in the closest association with Germany will it be possible for her to fulfil her external mission on
5 the Adriatic. . . . The German spirit must also penetrate and animate Austria's maritime development in the Mediterranean, so that we can be better prepared than hitherto for the developments of the future, which have already cast their shadow. . . . But however important for Austria German support in the east and
10 south may be, she has an equal need for the natural economic complement toward the north and west. The north German slope represents for Austria as much as for the rest of Germany the important transatlantic side of her world commerce. . . . It would be fatal to think that the German people will be satisfied with no
15 more than occasional measures promulgated by the Confederation regarding commerce, money, weights, measures and the enforcement of the judicial decisions of German courts in all the German states. It is rather a question of realising the idea of unity . . . in law, in economics, and in foreign relations by means of federal institu-
20 tions created for that purpose.

> Karl von Bruck (1860) *Die Aufgaben Oesterreichs* (Leipzig)
> quoted in T. S. Hamerow (1969) *The Social Foundations of German Unification 1858–71* (Princeton)

Questions

a Comment on Bruck's reference (lines 3–4) to the 'brisk rise of Austro–German commerce'.

b   What did Bruck mean by Austria's 'external mission on the Adriatic' (lines 4–5)?

c   What 'developments' had 'already cast their shadow' (lines 7–8)?

d   Discuss the significance of Bruck's thinking on 'the north German slope' (line 11).

e   Compare and contrast Bruck's conception of the proper function of the German Confederation with that of Bismarck outlined below.

4   Bismarck decries the German Confederation

Prussian interests completely coincide with those of most of the members of the Confederation, apart from Austria, but not with those of their governments, There is nothing more German than the development of Prussian particularist interests, rightly under-
5   stood. The policy of most of the governments . . . is opposed to ours, just because the existence and effective operation of the 33 governments outside Prussia and Austria, is the main obstacle to the strong evolution of Germany. Prussia would therefore be in no way disloyal to her German mission . . . if she ceased to attach any
10   considerable value to the sympathies of the *governments* of the medium sized states. . . .

     Moreover, experience leaves no doubt that . . . assurances of friendship are not the means whereby Prussia may suceed in living in a friendly, let alone secure, relationship with Austria. . . . Her
15   interests bid her combat and diminish Prussia's standing in Germany, so far as it lies within her power, and yet in the event of war, and against the multiplicity of dangers surrounding her, these same interests demand that she should be able to count on Prussia's full power for support. In this twofold need of Austria lies the only
20   means for Prussia to put herself on a clear and sure footing with the South German Great Power. . . .

     The relations of the two German Great Powers to each other would assume a different shape . . . if Prussia were to declare to Austria that, given the Confederation's present constitution and the
25   political tendency of the majority of its members, she would limit her participation to the strict execution of her clear obligations; that, beyond this, she would refuse to co-operate with the Confederation; any concession to the majority and to its President she would certainly decline. . . .

         Memorandum sent by Bismarck to Manteuffel, March 1858, in H. Kohl (ed.) *Bismarck Jahrbuch* vol ii (Berlin 1894–99) p 129

    a Explain Bismarck's claim (lines 1–2) that 'Prussia's interests coincide with those of most of the members of the Confederation ... but not with those of their governments'.

    b What justice was there in Bismarck's claim (lines 6–8) that the 'existence and effective operation of the 33 governments outside Prussia and Austria is the main obstacle to the strong evolution of Germany'?

    c To what extent are Bismarck's sentiments about Austria corroborated by other evidence in this chapter?

★   *d* What did Bismarck believe would be the nature of the change in Austro–Prussian relationships if his suggestions in the last paragraph (lines 24–29) were adopted?

    e What justification, if any, does Bismarck provide in this extract for his unyielding attitude towards Austria, and on what grounds does he believe Prussia can afford to adopt a stern line?

5 Prussia finds herself torn between friendship with France or Austria

The Council ... sitting today under my Chairmanship ... were agreed that France, with its unpredictable emperor, was the Power that was the source of danger to Europe, Germany and Prussia. ... The nearest ally to whom we have to look is obviously Germany.
5 She is as much affected by France's hankering after the left bank of the Rhine as Prussia. ... At first sight, it seems obvious that Prussia need make no special exertions in this direction, since federal help is reciprocal. Almost all Germany for the last 40 years has, however, cherished a hostile spirit against Prussia, and for a year this has been
10 decidedly on the increase. One must admit, therefore, the sad possibility that south Germany at any rate may seek to preserve its neutrality by means of separate negotiations with France and be defeated, whereupon the spectral fear that she is out to devour Germany would be laid for a long time to come. It is a matter,
15 then, of finding ways and means to put an end to German animosity against Prussia. By virtue of Prussia's superiority in moral and physical power, this would be easy if Austria, as our antagonist with her own emnity to us, were not also the moving spirit of German opposition. ... The necessity, therefore, arises
20 that we should enter into an undertanding with Austria such as would make such an extreme eventuality impossible.

    Agreement on this prevailed in the Council. Two decidedly different views, however, prevailed about the means to this end. The Minister von Schleinitz developed the view that, since he ...
25 recognised France as the source of danger, any intimate connection

with her in order to improve Prussia's position in Germany must be repudiated. Nothing then remained but to give up our hitherto sharp opposition to Austria and Germany, especially in the Federal *Diet* ... and then to bring about a defensive alliance with
30 Austria. ...

The remaining members of the Council declared themselves ... against such an alliance and also against any alteration of Prussia's German policy. Some even urged that Prussia's German policy should be taken to its logical conclusion, that she should not jib at a
35 breach between subjects and governments. (I declared myself most decidedly against this extreme course, for I will never play a part in Germany such as that played by Victor Emmanuel ...).

I give the following directive for our future policy. It is quite unnecessary to enter a special alliance with Austria for German
40 purposes. Should she request an alliance for non-German purposes, it should not be discussed until she actually faces an enemy that she is unable to withstand alone. ...

The Prince Regent William to Schleinitz, 26 March 1860,
(*Die Auswärtige Politik Preussens*, vol ii, part 1, no. 117)

Questions

★ *a* Why was the Emperor 'unpredictable' (line 2)?
  b Explain the 'hostile spirit' between Prussia and the remainder of Germany that had 'for a year ... been decidedly on the increase' (lines 9–10).
  c Comment on the 'spectral fear' that Prussia might devour Germany (line 13).
  d Should the Regent's assertion of Prussia's moral and physical power (lines 16–17) be dismissed as merely wishful thinking?
  e In what ways did Schleinitz find himself isolated in Council and why?
★ *f* What were the 'logical conclusions' of Prussia's German policy (line 34) and why did they prompt the Regent to compare his own role with that of King Victor Emmanuel?
  g Did the directive issued by the King mark a conclusive victory for one or other faction in the Council?

6 Prussia as an object of international derision

Prussia is always leaning on someone, always getting somebody to help her, never willing to help herself; always ready to deliberate, never to decide; present in congresses, but absent in battles; speaking and writing never for or against but only on the question;
5 ready to supply any amount of ideals or sentiments but shy of anything that savours of the actual. She has a large army, but

notoriously one in no condition for fighting. She is profuse in
circulars and notes, but generally has little to say for both sides. No
one counts her as a friend, no one dreads her as an enemy. How she
10 became a great power history tells us, why she remains so, nobody
can tell. ... Prussia unaided would not keep the Rhine or the
Vistula for a month from her ambitious neighbours.

The Times, 1860, quoted in H. Bohme, *op. cit.*

Questions

a What specific episodes might the author of this piece have been
alluding to by his comments in lines 1–2?
b What evidence was there for the assertion that the Prussian army
was 'notoriously one in no condition for fighting' (line 7)?
c Discuss the significance of the comments concerning the Rhine
and the Vistula (lines 11–12).
★ d What relationships may the tenor of this piece have to domestic
events in Prussia at this time?

7 The Eisenach Declaration of the *Nationalverein* August 1859

The present dangerous situation of Europe and of Germany and the
need to subordinate the demands of political parties to the great
common task of German unification have brought together from
the various German states a number of men ... for the purpose of
5 coming to an understanding about the establishment of a constitution for united Germany. ... They have agreed on the following
points:
1. In the present position of the world we see great dangers
threatening the independence of our German Fatherland – these are
10 increased rather than diminished by the peace just concluded
between France and Austria.
2. These dangers have their ultimate origin in the faulty constitution of Germany.
3. For this purpose it is necessary that the German Federal *Diet*
15 should be replaced by a firm, strong, permanent central government and that a German national assembly should be summoned.
4. In the present circumstances effective steps for the attainment of
this aim can originate only with Prussia. We shall, therefore, work
to the end that Prussia may take the initiative.
20 5. Should Germany in the immediate future be again directly
threatened from outside, the command of her military forces and
her diplomatic representation abroad shall be transferred to Prussia.
...
6. It is the duty of every German to support the Prussian govern-

25   ment according to his strength, in so far as its exertions are based
upon the assumption that the tasks of the Prussian state and the
tasks and needs of Germany coincide in essentials . . . .

7. We expect all patriots in the German Fatherland, whether they
belong to the democratic or to the constitutional party, to place
30   national independence and unity above party demands . . . .

> W. Mommsen (1960) *Deutsche Parteiprogramme* (Munich)
> p 131

Questions

   a Why was the present situation of Europe and Germany 'dangerous' (line 1)?

★ *b* What considerations could have induced people, other than
Prussians, to support the programme of the *Nationalverein*?

   c What was 'the peace just concluded between France and Austria'
(lines 10–11). Why should it have added to the perception of
danger?

   d Which institution is being especially singled out for condemna-
tion in point 2?

   e Why was Prussia being singled out as the single state capable of
taking 'effective steps for the attainment of this aim' (lines
17–18)?

   f Why should Germany 'in the immediate future be again directly
threatened from outside' (lines 20–21)?

   g Comment on the nature of the patriotic call being made in this
address.

8 Bavaria seeks a middle way

Bavaria desires to group the medium-sized German states round
herself and to negotiate with Prussia and Austria as the third
independent force, counted equal with them in Germany. . . . The
Bavarian government will be strengthened in . . . withstanding the
5   demands of Prussia, by the temper prevailing throughout the
whole country. No description can do justice to the antipathy to
Prussia prevailing in Bavaria. . . . The same spirit of hostility to
Prussia prevails in the upper and lower classes and I am bound to
say in former almost more than in the latter. Bavarian newspapers
10   exercise the greatest and most damaging influence in this connection. . . . This picture is a gloomy one, but . . . completely true and
well founded. There is no sympathy for Prussia in Bavaria, but
although we are not liked, thanks to the organisation of our
Prussian army, another feeling which had to some extent been lost
15   has again taken hold, that is, respect for Prussia. Despite all
Bavaria's hatred for Prussia, despite all her particularist selfishness,

if a danger of war from France loomed up tomorrow in Germany, she would certainly be ready to let herself be protected by Prussia and to trust herself unreservedly to Prussia's leadership.

> Landenburg (Prussian envoy in Munich) to Schleinitz, 9 November 1861, (*Die Auswärtige Politik Preussens*) vol ii, no. 419, p 490

Questions

    a What, according to the author, was Bavaria attempting to set up?

★ *b* Why should such a plan now be forthcoming?

    c What were the 'demands of Prussia' (line 5)?

    d Account for 'the antipathy to Prussia prevailing in Bavaria'? (lines 6–7).

    e Why had 'respect for Prussia' (line 15) 'to some extent lost . . . again taken hold'?

★ *f* Comment on the reference (lines 13–14) to the organisation of the Prussian army.

IV Military Budgets, Constitutional Crisis and the Bismarckian Vision

The revival of Liberal fortunes in Prussia only mirrored a plethora of others in Europe. In France, Napoleon III made serious efforts to inaugurate his vaunted 'liberal empire' while the Garibaldian conquests of 1860 gave Liberal Nationalists a glorious, if shortlived, vision of the future which awaited them. But Prussia's liberalism was torn apart in late 1861 by the conflict between the King and his parliament over military reform.

The nature of the reforms themselves quickly became less significant as the intensity of the power struggle increased. The regent, who succeeded his brother in 1860, wanted a stronger army. This in itself was not especially contentious: memories of Prussia's humiliation at Olmutz lingered in many minds and Prussia, with a population of about 18000000, had an anomalous system of draft which regularly resulted in about a third of the theoretically eligible young men not being called up. This was widely acceptable to the *Landtag* when it was first discussed there in February 1860. The problems were over the increased length of service (from two years to three) which the Liberals objected to purely on grounds of expense, and especially the proposed changes to the *Landwehr*. This territorial body was felt by Roon, the brilliant new Minister for War, to be peopled almost exclusively by men neither young nor without prior domestic ties. He proposed an expansion of the regular army which would make the status of the *Landweher* more sinecurial by comparison.

It was this which incensed the Liberals, who saw in the *Landwehr* an effective alternative to the Frederician style of Prussian militarism. In seeking to demote it, the king and Roon were seen in fact to be removing a possible impediment to the total control of the army by the Crown. When the Liberals proposed amendments, the government outmanoeuvred all parliamentary opposition, using the old Army Laws from 1814 which were felt to provide an adequate grounds to introduce the reforms anyway, since they stipulated the king as Commander in Chief of Prussian Forces. The Lower House had simply to vote funds. This they did for one year in May 1860 with a rider to the effect that all their objections to the reforms should be met. This was ignored and the new regiments were created.

Liberals anger was now intense, especially on the left wing of the Party, anyway disenchanted by the absence of constructive moves towards unification and the oligarchical nature of government in Prussia. A large splinter faction set themselves up as the Progressives (*Fortschrittspartei*), gaining 110 seats in the elections in December 1861. The largest single group in the Lower House, they insisted on a detailed budget analysis as a means of pre-empting the king from continuing his reforms. He thereupon dissolved parliament, leaving the rump of moderate Liberal ministers torn between the forces of reaction from the king and the military and the apparent recklessness of the Progressives. Their place was taken by Conservative Ministers, anxious quickly to resolve the affair.

But the Progressives won 135 seats in the elections of May 1862. In fact, by this point the remaining contention (the reduction of three years' service to two) was agreed by all parties, except the king. Since the Lower House refused to vote further sums for army reorganisation in the face of his intransigence, the debate was now entirely a constitutional one. The king was clearly prepared to abdicate, though his son the Crown Prince advocated a climb down while the former Head of Government, Manteufel pressed for a dictatorship using the military. It was in this impase that the king, purely on the recommendation of von Roon, recalled Bismarck from Paris and invited him to head the Government.

The historian A. J. P. Taylor has observed that of all one might say of Bismarck at this stage, he had no set plans whatever for German unification. Indeed, the initiative lay much more with Austria. Although, in the wake of her defeat by the French in 1859, she had lapsed briefly into reaction – to the benefit of *kleindeutsch* proponents in Prussia, the new Chief Minister Schmerling had, from February 1861, set up a parliament for the entire Austrian Empire in Vienna. From there he pressed for reform of the German Confederation and all hopes for a *Grossdeutschland* focused on Austria, rather than Prussia unless the latter were suddenly to become dominated by middle-class Liberals. The pre-eminence of the *Junker* class made that seem most unlikely.

Bismarck's was in many ways an extraordinary appointment, albeit in an extraordinary situation. The king distrusted Bismarck's outspokeness and was probably only persuaded by Bismarck's promise to see through the task entrusted to him by the king on 22 September 1862. Anxious not least that Prussia's enemies and rivals should not gain too much capital from her discomfiture, Bismarck at once withdrew the budget proposals for 1863 in an effort to appease the Lower House. He could not persuade the king better than his predecessors to change his mind over the length of service, but his notorious 'blood and iron' speech was, it is sometimes argued, merely a misdirected attempt to persuade the Liberals of his exciting plans if they could only break the constitutional deadlock.

The Progressives spurned him, and Bismarck lost patience. As his speech to the Lower House early in 1862 intimated, he had institutional support and he was prepared to rule without Parliament – which he prorogued in October 1863. A theoretical basis for such a radical action was easily found; it did not necessarily have to convince.

1 The programme of the Prussian *Volksverein* 1861

The undersigned ... proclaim their intention of influencing the coming elections in their favour, and further, of creating for all like-minded men in the Prussian people a focus ... thereby offering a hand to like-minded men in the wider German fatherland. They
5 have agreed ...:
1. Unity of our German fatherland, yet not *like the Kingdom of Italy by blood and fire* but by the *union of our princes and people* and by holding firm to authority and right. ... *No decline into the dirt of a German republic. No theft of crowns and cheats of nationality.*
10 2. No break with the past internally within our state. No abandonment of its Christian foundation. ... No ... weakening of the army. ... No parliamentary rule and no ministerial responsibility established by a constitution. Personal rule by divine and not by constitutional right. Church marriages, Christian schools, Christian
15 authority. ...
3. Protection and proper regard for honourable work, for all property, all rights and all classes. No favour for, or exclusive domination by, money wealth. ...

W. Mommsen (1960) *Deutsche Parteiprogramme* (Munich) p 45

Questions

★ a What made the 'coming elections' (line 2) unusually tense ones?
  b Comment upon the dismissive language used to describe a German republic (lines 8–9).
  c Explain the reference to the 'theft of crowns and cheats of nationality' (line 9).
  d Why was particular mention made to the Army (line 12)?
  e Discuss the reference made to 'money wealth' (line 18).

2 The foundation programme of the *Fortschrittspartei* [Progressive Party] June 1861

We are united in our loyalty to the King and in the firm conviction that the constitution is the indissoluble bond which holds Prince and people together. ...

We are equally clear that Prussia's existence and greatness depend
5 upon a firm unification of Germany, which cannot be conceived
without a strong Central Executive Power in the hands of Prussia
or without a common German representative assembly. . . .

For the honour and power of our Fatherland, no sacrifice will
ever be too great. But for the sake of the sustained pursuit of . . .
10 war, the greatest economy in the peacetime military budget seems
to us essential. We are convinced that the maintenance of the militia
. . . increased conscription of men capable of bearing arms, the two-
year period of service – all these offer a guarantee that the Prussian
people in arms will be fully qualified for war.
15 It must be abundantly clear . . . that the attainment of these aims
will remain a pious hope so long as a thorough reform of the
present Upper House has not been achieved. . . .

W. Mommsen (1960) *Deutsche Partiprogramme* (Munich)
p 133

Questions

a Compare and contrast the conception of kingship (lines 1–3)
with those of the *Volksverein* and the *Nationalverein*.
b Comment on the Progressives' chosen role for Prussia (lines
4–14).
c Do the three party programmes share any common objectives?
★ d Why did the Party choose to select the issue of military
expenditure for specific comment?

3 Protocol for an alliance between Austria and the medium–sized states against Prussia

In consideration of the ever more threatening posture of affairs in
Europe, and particularly in Germany, [we] . . . set out the following views and proposals as guidelines. . . .
1. The Imperial and Royal Government [of Austria] and the Royal
5 Government of Württemberg will agree to no project for the
reform of the Confederation which would exclude Austria from
the bonds of the common German constitution and subject the rest
of the German princes to any one member of the Confederation.
. . . They adhere to the preservation of Austria's position and the
10 equality of Württemberg and of the other big states in the Confederation as the condition of any reform of the federal constitution. . . . [They] will, therefore, also oppose any proposal by which
the diplomatic and military leadership of the federal states would be
shared between any two federal governments. . . .
15 6. The two governments will, through their envoys in Berlin,
present identical notes [to Prussia] in which they will indicate that

the [Prussian] plan for the reform of the Germanic Confederation . . .
is incompatible with the basic law and forms of the Confederation.
The notes will also express a confident expectation that the Royal
20 Prussian Government will give the plan no further consideration. . . .

> Darmstadt, 29 January 1862, *Staatsarchiv, Staatsministerium,*
> Konv. 46 Fasc. 3, quoted in H. Böhm (1971) *The Founda-*
> *tion of the German Empire* (Oxford University Press)

Questions

a Why was the 'posture of affairs in Europe and particularly in
Germany' (lines 1–2) seen as 'ever more threatening'?
b Was the notion of sharing diplomatic and military leadership of
the federal states (lines 12–14) ever seriously entertained?
c What was understood to be meant by 'the basic law and forms
of the Confederation' (line 18)?
★ *d* How confident in reality was the expectation that Prussia at
this point would now drop her ideas for reform of the German
Confederation (lines 19–20)?

4   Anticipating a crisis

According to my innermost conviction, the country will remain
entirely quiet during this dissolution, but the new house will be
composed of even more democratic elements, if that is possible,
and if, as I fear, there will be no compromise in the army question,
5   then in three months we will have another dissolution and at the
end a change in the electoral law with a reactionary ministry or the
entire abolition of the chamber. . . .

> Gerson Bleichröder in a letter to Baron James in Paris, 11
> March 1862, quoted in Fritz Stern (1977) *Gold and Iron*
> (George Allen & Unwin)

Questions

a What might Bleichröder have understood by 'even more democratic elements' (line 3)?
b How far does this source corroborate or contradict that of
Károlyi in extract 6 below?

5   Cassel veers towards favouring a Franco–
Prussian commercial treaty

Opinion in this country, now, alas, under the Liberal Party who are
setting the tone, is decidedly in favour of the conclusion of the

treaty. It sees in it both commercial and political advantages – to be derived from the more intimate connection with Prussia. For that reason most of the industrialists of the country . . . stated that they were not afraid of French competition and must therefore declare themselves in favour of the lowering of customs duties and the maximum of free trade, which would open the French market to their products.

As far as the Government of this country is concerned, there are many reasons for its hesitation . . . both of an economic and a political nature. . . . The iron industries, controlled by Cassel, which will suffer damage from French competition, especially arouse its anxiety. It is, however, the political side of the treaty that must weigh most in the balance and hold the Government back from over-hasty decisions. In the present circumstances there is, on one side, the fear of antagonizing Prussia; on the other, the consciousness of belonging together with her within the confines of the *Zollverein*. This feeling is so important and any dissolution of the latter is considered likely to bring such damage upon this country, that the Government is very perplexed over this urgent decision. . . .

> Karnicky (Austrian envoy in Cassel) to Rechberg, 25 April 1862, (Vienna, *Haus-Hof-und-Staatsarchiv*, PA VII, no. 81)

Questions

a Discuss the political advantages which Cassel might derive from the signing of a Franco–Prussian commercial treaty (lines 3–4).

b Discuss the motives of the industrialists in their support of such a treaty. Were they exclusively commercial (lines 5–9)?

★ c What were the risks, politically and economically, for Cassel in 'antagonizing Prussia' (line 17)?

d Why was the decision for Cassel whether or not to support this treaty an urgent one (lines 16–19)?

6 Constitutional crisis in Berlin

When one surveys the phases through which Prussian domestic politics have passed since the beginning of the ministerial crisis, one's observations on these matters relate partly to the resignation of the previous ministry and partly to the governmental tendencies . . . underlying the newly formed Cabinet. . . .

Concerning the new direction the Prussian government is to take . . . it consists in reconciliation with moderate Conservatism – the maintenance of an Upper House supporting the government – an attempt to obtain as favourable an outcome of the elections as possible by the influence . . . of government officials.

If, nevertheless, the elections do not succeed (which is, alas, probable) ... the Lower House will be dissolved again ... and a new electoral law enacted by decree.

15 Even in the political course on which he has by now embarked, the king is willing to attempt to carry on the government with loyal, independent men, attached to *him* personally and to no-one else ... He is willing to derive as much profit as possible from those in the country still of a 'monarchical' persuasion in order to protect and hold firm the inalienable rights of the Crown against the

20 invasion of democracy. He will attempt to do this without a *coup d'état*, or at least by avoiding any proceeding violating the constitution as a whole, to which he has sworn loyalty. He will seek a form of state dependent on a representative parliament, and the maintenance of freedom – yet freedom distinct from that of the Manteuffel

25 régime. ...

In every circumstance, the new phase can be considered an incontestably better course for the future. ... If democracy is suppressed inside Prussia, its damaging influence on the rest of Germany will also be crippled. ...

> Károlyi (Austrian envoy in Berlin) to Rechberg, 22 March 1862, (Vienna, *Haus-Hof-und Staatsarchiv*, PA III, no 75)

Questions

a   What were the 'phases through which Prussian domestic politics' had 'passed since the beginning of the ministerial crisis' (lines 1–2)?

b   What preconditions were likely to be necessary for the Upper House to support the government (lines 6–10)?

★ c   Comment on the likely nature of 'a new electoral law enacted by decree' (lines 12–13).

d   How likely was it, according to what one may infer from the extract, that the king would be able to 'carry on the government' yet stay within the Constitution?

e   Discuss the notion of 'the maintenance of freedom' (lines 23–24) as revealed in this passage.

★ f   To what extent is this passage helpful as a means of understanding the assumptions of Austrian diplomacy at this time?

7   A British perspective

Monsieur de Bismarck might be described as [firstly] Prussian, [secondly] through and through Prussian and [thirdly] German through Prussian.

5 It may perhaps serve usefully to characterise this gentleman, if I state to your lordship my entire conviction of his high honour and

integrity, that he has a great, perhaps undue, contempt of public opinion, and hardly less of German liberalism and its leaders, that he is frank to the verge of imprudence, in expressing his opinions, and has extraordinary command of temper. I think however that
10   scarcely any considerations would weigh with him against the perspective of a territorial rounding off, for Prussia, which is the object of his life, and political aspirations, and it is on this account that his position in Paris might, in certain contingencies, become fraught with danger to the peace of Europe. . . .

> Sir Arthur Malet to Lord John Russell (Foreign Secretary), 28 May 1862 (London PRO, FO 30/201)

Questions

a   Discuss the assessment made of Bismarck in lines 1–3 of this passage. Was it prophetic or borne out by Bismarck's conduct at this point?
b   'His high honour and integrity' (lines 5–6). How apt was this observation?
c   What was understood at this point by a 'territorial rounding off of Prussia' (line 11)?
d   Why might Bismarck's position in Paris 'become fraught with danger to the peace of Europe' (lines 13–14)?

8   A furious letter from the King of Prussia

War to the death against the monarch and his standing army has been vowed, and in order to reach that goal, the Progressivists and Democrats and ultra-Liberals scorn no means . . . the shortening of the term of service is demanded so that firm, well disciplined
5   military training, the effects of which will hold during the long period of leave, shall not be given the soldier. The under-officers shall become officers, not as everyone could in Prussia since 1808 by passing one and the same examination, but without proving this equality of cultural level, so that a schism will develop in the
10   officers' corps and dissatisfaction will slowly creep into them and the Democrats will be able to develop an officers' caste of their own which, because they are neither trained nor steeled in their views to stand loyally by the throne, are to be won for the revolution. Since loyalty and self-sacrifice for king and throne are to be expected
15   from the present officers and through them to be transferred to the troops, therefore the officers' class is slandered in every possible way, and then one wonders that the officers are angry? And even censures them for this!

'A people's army [behind] Parliament'. That is the solution
20   revealed since *Frankfurt am Main* [a reference to a speech by

Schulze-Delitsch] to which I counter with the watchword: 'A disciplined army that is also the people in arms, [behind] the king the warlord'.

Between these two watchwords no agreement is possible.

King William of Prussia to the Liberal von Saucken Julienfelde, August 1862, quoted in E. N. Anderson (1954) *The Social and Political Conflict in Prussia, 1858–1864* (University of Nebraska)

Questions

a Was the king exaggerating the scale of the threat posed by Liberal opposition to his army reforms in his references to the 'war to the death' that the controversy had now reached (line 1)?

b Discuss the reference (lines 3–4) to the 'shortening of the service'. Who advocated this and what did those who opposed it intend to substitute in its place?

★ c Explain the reference in line 7 to the army reforms of 1808.

d What was William scornfully indicating in his prediction that 'Democrats will . . . develop an officer caste of their own' (line 11)?

e Why was the king so adamant that there could be no reconciling the two slogans of 'A people's army [behind] Parliament' (line 19) and his own 'A disciplined army . . .' (lines 21–22)?

9 The limited impact of Prussia's internal problems

Count Rechberg has too much penetration to be able to believe that the war which he is waging against us both on the commercial and political field, although . . . initially successful, will oblige us to abandon our standpoint and to go over to the uncertain Austrian
5 position. He is too precisely acquainted with the exact political, financial and economic position of present day Austria and knows too surely that it is not hidden from us, to reckon on the sustained operation of the present false attitude of some of the German governments and of public opinion in south Germany or to connect
10 with it the hope of lasting success.

He may delude himself about the effect of our present domestic difficulties upon our differences with Austria. Yet here too it is hard to mistake the truth. Whatever turn the crisis, caused by the strong feeling of the Opposition in the present Lower House, may
15 take, in no event will it bring us closer to another view of the unrestrained hostility to Prussia in which Austria is at present indulging. As far as our commercial policy is immediately con-

cerned, there exists among us no difference of opinion worth
taking into account as to the cold and inconsiderate way in which
20 Austria is acting. She is endangering our interests through her
aggression instead of protecting hers. ... Should Austria wish in
fact for what is constructive and possible ... she has gone sadly
wrong in the choice of her present means. ...

In essentials, the same is exactly true of the purely political field.
25 If Austria wishes to have in us, on any hypothesis, a willing partner
in the counsels of the European Powers and a companion in arms in
a European war, she must put an end to her agitation against us and
her suspicion of us. She must ... clear existing difficulties out of
the way in co-operation with us. ... She must begin to respect not
30 only our equality of status and essential equality of rights, but to
acknowledge them and to react accordingly. On such preliminary
conditions ... *we are ready*, as we have always been, *for an
understanding* and we believe we are not mistaken in saying that the
gain from such an understanding would be *at least* as much on the
35 Austrian side as on ours and that further persistence of the present
quarrel must become *injurious to the whole of Germany*. ...

> Bernstorff to Werther (Prussian envoy in Vienna), 25
> September 1862, (*Die Auswärtige Politik Preussens*, vol ii,
> part 2, no. 493, p 757)

Questions

a What was the war Rechberg was alleged to be waging 'on the
commercial and political field' (lines 2–3)?
b Discuss the 'present false attitude of some of the German
governments' (lines 8–9).
c Why might Rechberg be likely to delude himself over Prussia's
'present domestic difficulties' (lines 11–12)?
★ d What was the European War Prussia had in mind for which
Austria might seek assistance (line 27)?
e Consider what Prussia understood by 'equality of status and
essential equality of rights' (line 30) and what good reasons, if
any, led Austria to be loath to grant them.
f What kind of '*understanding*' was Prussia prepared to enter
in with Austria (line 33)? Is the italicisation of this term
(reproduced from the original) in any way significant?
g Is there a hidden message in the notion that 'further persistence
of the present quarrel must become *injurious to the whole of
Germany*' (line 36)?
h Despite being addressed to Werther, is there any sense in which
this document may have been intended to reach a wider
audience? If so, to whom?

10 Blood and iron

A misuse of constitutional powers could happen on any side, and would lead to a reaction from the other side. The crown, for example, could dissolve [the *Landtag*] a dozen times, and that would certainly be in accordance with the letter of the Constitu-
5 tion, but it would be a misuse. In the same way, it can challenge the budget cancellations as much as it likes: but the limit is difficult to set; shall it be set at 6 000 000 or 16 000 000 or 60 000 000? There are members of the National Union, a party respected because of the justice of its demands, highly esteemed members, who considered
10 all standing armies superfluous. Now, what if a National Assembly were of this opinion! Wouldn't the Government have to reject it? People speak of the 'sobriety' of the Prussian people. Certainly, the great independence of the individual makes it difficult in Prussia to rule with the constitution; in France it is different, the independence
15 of the individual is lacking there.

A constitutional crisis is not shameful, but honourable. Further-more, we are perhaps too 'educated' to put up with a constitution; we are too critical; the ability to judge government measures and bills of the National Assembly is too widespread. ... We are too
20 ardent, we like to carry too heavy a weight of armour for our fragile bodies: but we should also make use of it. Germany doesn't look to Prussia's liberalism, but to its power: Bavaria, Württem-berg, Baden can indulge in liberalism, but no one will expect them to undertake Prussia's role; Prussia must gather and consolidate her
25 strength in readiness for the favourable moment, which has already been missed several times; Prussia's boundaries according to the Vienna treaties are not favourable to a healthy political life; not by mean of speeches and majority verdicts will the great decisions of the time be made – that was the great mistake of 1848 and 1849 –
30 but by iron and blood. ...

> Bismarck on 29 September 1862 to the budget commission of the Prussian *Landtag*, quoted by W. N. Medlicott and D. K. Coveney (eds) (1971) in *Bismarck and Europe* (Ed-ward Arnold)

Questions

a What point was Bismarck attempting to drive home in his observations about those members of the National Union who opposed a standing army (lines 8–10)?

b Discuss the underlying meaning of Bismarck's claim that 'a constitutional crisis is not shameful, but honourable' (line 16).

c How fair was the assertion in 1862 (lines 21–22) that Germany doesn't look to Prussia's liberalism, but to its power'?

d   When had the 'favourable moment' already been missed 'several times' (lines 25–26)?

e   What justice was there in Bismarck's claim that Prussia's boundaries, decided by the Vienna Treaties were 'not favourable to a healthy political life' (line 27)?

11   Spelling out home truths

Rights are claimed for the Lower House which it either does not possess at all or shares [with the king and Upper House]. If you, gentleman, by your decision alone, had the right to fix the budget finally ... the right to request from His Majesty the King the
5   dismissal of ministers who did not have your confidence; the right to fix the size and organisation of the army by means of your decisions over the state's expenditure; the right, which you do not have according to the constitution, but claim in the address, to control definitively the relations between the state's executive
10 power and its officials – if you had these rights you would in fact be in possession of full power to govern this country.

Your address rests on the basis of these claims. ... I believe therefore that I can characterise its practical significance in a few words. This address requires that the royal Hohenzollern House
15 should surrender its constitutional right to govern and transfer it to the majority of this House of Parliament. You invest the demand with the form of a declaration that the constitution is violated when the Crown and the Upper House do not conform to your will. Your reproach of having violated the constitution is directed
20 against the Ministry, not against the Crown. ...

You know as well as anyone in Prussia that the Ministry acts in Prussia in the name of, and at the behest of, His Majesty the King and that it put through these very acts of government, in which you claim to see a violation of the constitution, in his name and at
25 his behest ... a Prussian ministry is different from an English one. An English ministry ... is a parliamentary ministry ... but we are ministers of His Majesty the King. ...

You find the ground for the violation of the constitution specifically in Article 99 [which] runs ... 'All income and expendi-
30 ture of the State must for each year be proposed in advance and set out in the State budget'. If this were followed by the words 'which is annually fixed by the Lower House' you would be completely right in the grievances you state. ... But there follows in the text: '... [the budget] will be fixed annually by means of a law'. Article
35 62 states with unanswerable clarity how a law is enacted ... that for the enactment of a law, for the budget law as for any other, the concurrence of the Crown and the two Houses of Parliament is required. This article, moreover, mentions particularly that the

Upper House is entitled to reject a budget decided upon by the
40 Lower House but not agreeable to itself.
    The Constitution lacks any stipulation as to which of them shall
give way if no agreement is reached between the three powers. . . .
The Constitution then refers to compromise as the way to an
understanding. A statesman, experienced in constitutional govern-
45 ment has said that life under a Constitution is at any time a series of
compromises. If the effort to reach compromise is made fruitless by
one of the participating powers seeking to carry its point of view
with doctrinaire absolutism, then the series of compromises is
interrupted and in its place conflict enters, and because the life of
50 the State cannot stand still, conflicts become questions of power.
          Speech of Bismarck in the Prussian Lower House, 27
          January 1863, (Bismarck, *Gesammelte Werke*, vol X, p 153)

Questions

a '. . . the right to fix the size and organization of the army . . .'
   (lines 5–6). Why was this particular issue specified by Bismarck
   in his address?
b Was Bismarck's assertion that the Lower House was claiming
   'to control definitively the relationship between the State's
   executive power and its officials' (lines 8–10) a fair representation of events?
c What grounds did Bismarck furnish for his claim that, in
   opposing the budget put forward by the ministers, the Lower
   House were in fact opposing the Crown (lines 21–27)?
d Paraphrase, in your own words, the essence of Bismarck's
   argument concerning Article 99 and Article 62.
e Why was it that the Constitution 'lacks any stipulation as to
   which of them shall then give way' (lines 41–42)?
f What was Bismarck's underlying intention in discussing the role
   of compromise and 'questions of power' (line 50)? Is the style of
   his address a conciliatory one?

V The Danish Problem and Austro–Prussian Rapprochement

At the opening of Parliament in 1863, Bismarck's political demise, rather than any imminent call to arms, seemed most plausible. Liberal hostility persisted, both against the budget but also the Alvensleben Convention whereby he promised assistance in putting down the rebellion in Russian Poland. Although the resonance and importance of the Liberals has attracted considerable scholarly controversy, Bismarck cannot have been pleased when in October 1863 they won another substantial majority in the general election.

But the ability of the Liberals meaningfully to oppose Bismarck was undermined by the nature of his successes in both foreign and economic policy. In the latter, his preference for *laissez-faire* capitalism accorded well with theirs. The reopening of the Schleswig-Holstein question also saw the first critical schism open up for the Liberals. The Treaty of London in 1852 had eased tension, but certainly not removed the source of it. When Frederick VII in 1863 created a single constitution for Schleswig and Denmark, he may have been relying on existing tensions between Prussia and Austria to tide over an undoubted breach of the 1852 Treaty. He himself died shortly after, but not before the German pretender, Frederick of Augustenburg, proclaiming himself the Duke of Schleswig-Holstein, inflamed German nationalists.

Prussia, no more than Austria, wanted Augustenburg to be successful, and yet both powers had to pay at least nominal regard to the German confederation. In this situation, Bismarck acted with studious caution, in co-operation with Austria. Their efforts to dissuade Confederate enthusiasm for Augustenburg were frustrated when he unilaterally installed an unofficial 'court' in Holstein. In January 1864, therefore, the Austro–Prussian Convention was signed and troops entered Schleswig, quickly defeating the Danes at Düppel. At the London Conference two months later, King Christian IX of Denmark was utterly intransigent, however, and refused to accept the autonomy of Schleswig. Denmark, despite the promises of Lord Palmerston to the contrary, found herself isolated from the Great Powers. Within a week of the expiry of the armistice in June 1864, Austria and Prussia had routed them and forced the surrender of both duchies.

Whatever the tortuous complexities of Bismarck's policies over the next two years, he aimed always to ensure that Schleswig and Holstein would both come to Prussia. The Augustenburg claim was now defunct, in the wake of the London Conference, and Austria faced increasingly onerous economic problems. To some extent, this encouraged a gradualist approach from Bismarck. Relations, though strained, only seriously deteriorated when the Prussian Finance Ministry blocked Austrian negotiations with the *Zollverein*.

This left both Austria and Prussia with a dilemma about their future relationship. Pouilly-Mensdorff, the new Foreign Minister in Vienna, looked for an understanding with France to check Prussian plans of expansion, and woo medium-sized states to herself as well. The two duchies would become a state in the Confederation on their own account with a sovereign government. Bismarck, predictably, vehemently opposed such a plan, but he did not want Austria to leave the alliance, and argued against the wishes of the king and most of the Prussian Crown Council for a conciliatory policy. The result of this was the compromise of Bad Gastein. Here the Austrians successfully insisted on the continued joint sovereignty of Austria and Prussia over the two duchies.

Considerable controversy has attached to Bismarck's role here as a 'pacifier'. Certainly he was acutely aware that a war with Austria would need money which might well not be forthcoming from the *Landtag*. But even after early summer when it was clear that in fact the means for a year-long campaign had been raised, he still sought an accommodation with Austria – influenced perhaps especially by the belief that Austria's plight (financially) was sufficiently serious that, properly handled, she might concede a great deal more. Certainly, there is a plethora of evidence against seeing Bismark, between 1863 and 1865, as in any sense 'resolved' upon war with Austria.

1   Free elections?

To the royal Prussian voters of the manor Meffersdorf, Schwerta and Volkersdorf. His Majesty our most gracious king and sovereign has commanded that on the 20th of this month the election should take place, and has pronounced that the election will be free
5   only if the choice falls on such persons who will vote in accordance with the disposition and will of His Majesty and his ministers. . . . I have commanded that those voters who act to the contrary shall, if they are workers in the forest or on the estates, be dismissed, and that the same procedure shall be followed in the brickworks, the
10   peat banks and the factory for ovenware and pottery; that the supervisory personnel of the forest, the estate, the garden, the mill, the bakery, and the sawmill shall be given notice. . . . I demand of all the above mentioned voters who have any sort of connection with me that they participate in the election on the 20th of this

15   month. Whoever has not brought to me personally a satisfactory
excuse for staying away shall be treated in the same way as those
voters who on the 20th of this month give their vote to such
electors who ... will again choose the present members of the
legislature or choose such members who will vote in the new lower
20   house against the will of His Majesty and his ministers.

> Estate owner in Lauban in Silesia in an announcement to
> his tenantry, 1863, quoted by Theodore S. Hamerow
> (1969) in *The Social Foundations of German Unification 1858–
> 1871* (Princeton)

Questions

a   '... such persons who will vote in accordance with the disposition and will of His Majesty and his ministers' (lines 5–6). Who
were these persons?

b   Who were 'the present members of the legislature' (lines 18–19)?

★ c   In what political circumstances did this election take place?

★ d   How wide was the franchise at this time?

2   Leaving aside the question of trade

I have drawn the attention of the Imperial [Austrian] Ambassador
(who fully acknowledges, as I do, the great importance of trust and
sincerity between our respective Cabinets) to the fact that friendly
relations between us cannot be attained more easily, or be more
5   securely safeguarded, than by striving first of all for similarity of
views and aspirations in the *purely political* field. I said that an
understanding here could be reached without impairing the independent development, which each state is obliged to assure to the
special and established interests of its subjects in the economic field.
10   I observed that to mix the two matters – to transfer commercial and
industrial interests to the political field or contrariwise – might
make a sincere understanding more difficult. ...

> Bismarck to Werther (Prussian Ambassador in Vienna), 9
> April 1863, (Merseburg, Deutsches Zentralarchiv, AA II,
> Rep. 6, no. 1195)

Questions

a   What does Bismarck imply in his reference to 'the *purely political*
field' (line 6)?

b   '... independent development which each state is obliged to
assure' (lines 7–8). Was this true in the case of *each* state?

c   How plausible was Bismarck's determination not 'to mix the
two matters' (line 10)?

3   Together they stand

The position of the Imperial Austrian and Royal Prussian governments is fixed by the treaty which both, in common with France, Great Britain, Russia and Sweden, concluded with the Crown of Denmark on 8 May 1852 in London, after preliminary terms had
5   been determined in discussions with Denmark during the year 1851–2. Both governments consider these agreements, taken together, an inseparable whole to which the London Treaty provided the concluding piece. Now that the event, which this treaty envisaged, has actually occurred, both governments are
10   ready to execute the treaty, if the Crown of Denmark on its side carries out the preliminary terms of 1851–2. Their implementation formed the condition precedent of the signature of the London Treaty by Austria and Prussia. . . .

> Circular despatch of Bismarck to the Prussian envoys at the German Courts, 29 November 1863, (O. von Bismarck *Gesammelte Werke*, vol iv, no. 174, p 220)

Questions

★   a   What did the London Treaty attempt to resolve?
    b   What was 'the event, which this treaty envisaged' which 'has actually occurred' (lines 9–10)?
    c   What was the diplomatic significance of the announcement contained in this extract?

4   In defence of the monarchic principle

We consider the Danish conflict as essentially an episode in the fight of the monarchic principle against European revolution. We take our rule of conduct in handling the duchies' problem from our good appreciation of its effect upon that great question of the day.
5   If the good understanding between the monarchs of Prussia and Austria and their active energy can satisfy justifiable national needs, that is, those felt by the respectable sections of the nation, the revolution will be deprived of the pretexts from which it draws its strength. From the outset the present Prussian government has
10   been guided by this conviction in its handling of the Danish question. Up to now, our success has been according to our wishes, and I am convinced that in Vienna, as well as here, the good influence which the two German Powers have exercised over the public situation in Germany as a whole, by their common and
15   energetic action, will be felt. A glance at the present situation of Germany, compared with what it was six months ago, is sufficient to enable one to appreciate it. We believe we may also record with

satisfaction a substantial progress of Conservative feeling within both monarchies. In Germany this is a matter not merely of public opinion, as it finds its expression in the daily newspapers. The position of the German governments themselves has become essentially different and they are now no longer in danger of being driven into the current of revolution. . . .

We have found a bond in this joint action on the military and political fields of whose firmness and permanency we are convinced.

This is great progress, its significance goes far beyond the present moment, and we record it with satisfaction.

But the *decisive* success has not yet been attained and our work has not reached a conclusion. In order to make firm the position gained, we need a conclusive and lasting success. . . . All old quarrels will find new nourishment in the complaints each is making against the other and anarchy will once more raise its head in Germany, while trust and respect abroad, which depend upon the solid combination of Austria and Prussia, will again be lost, if people are not convinced that the two Powers, when united, face foreign powers aware of their unity and sufficiently conscious of their strength. . . .

> Bismarck to Werther (Prussian Ambassador in Vienna), 14 June 1864, (*Die Auswärtige Politik Preussens*, vol v, no. 147, p 220)

Questions

a Discuss the idea of 'the fight of the monarchic principle against European revolution' (lines 1–2).
b Comment on Bismarck's notion of 'justifiable national needs' (line 6) in the context of the Danish conflict.
c What were 'the pretexts' from which 'the revolution . . . draws its strength' (lines 8–9)?
★ d 'Up to now, our success has been according to our wishes' (lines 11–12). To what was Bismarck referring?
e What was meant by 'the good influence which the two German Powers have exercised over the public situation in Germany as a whole' (lines 12–14)?
f Comment on the 'substantial progress of conservative feeling within both monarchies' (lines 18–19).

5 The power of Prussia and Austria in harness

A true German and Conservative policy is only possible when Austria and Prussia are united and take the lead. . . . We consider combination, though it is true both Powers and even all Germany

already owe important successes to it, from the wider standpoint
5 than that of the moment and as the means to consolidate the
successes we have won. We consider combination (such as the joint
action in waging war which is our immediate political purpose) as
the foundation of an enduring unity . . . and we have seen Austria's
welcoming response in the same light. . . . If Prussia and Austria are
10 not united, politically Germany does not exist. . . . This natural
relationship existed to a certain extent before 1848. Unfortunately
events have since caused it to be almost forgotten. Quarrelling
between Austria and Prussia has left some of the smaller states
unsure, and made others presumptuous. . . .
15   If we hesitate or weaken . . . timidity or disunity will be thought
to impair our resolution. Courage will be found for majority
decisions, to which we *cannot* conform, and the collapse of Germany will be brought about by an absurd effort to cause the
European policy of two monarchs, powerful and victorious in
20 arms, to be taken along in the wake of a few, unarmed small states
whose whole significance consists in the misdirected courage of
their Parliaments and newspapers. If, on the contrary, we come
forward firmly . . . they will conform as soon as they see the firm
will of Austria and Prussia. . . .

> Bismarck to Werther (Prussian Ambassador in Vienna), 6
> August 1864, (O. von Bismarck, *Gesammelte Werke*, vol iv,
> no. 454, p 525)

Questions

a 'We consider combination . . . as the foundation of an enduring
   unity' (lines 6–8). Does this amount to a repudiation – from
   Bismarck's own mouth – of *kleindeutschland*?
b How fair is Bismarck's observation that Austrian and Prussian
   quarrels had made several smaller states 'presumptuous'?
★ c Assess Bismarck's motives for calling here for closer links
   between Austria and Prussia.

6 To return to trade . . .

[Prussia] adheres to her repeatedly expressed view that the entry of
the Imperial state [Austria] into the *Zollverein* is for both sides, in
practice, unrealisable. Neither this view nor other considerations,
however, preclude us from believing that a considerable *rapproche-*
5 *ment* to be possible, in commercial policy, between Austria and the
Zollverein. We see no hindrance to such a *rapprochement* in our treaty
with France. On the contrary we believe that on the basis of that
treaty, further reliefs and stimulation could very reasonably be
afforded to trade with Austria. . . . As far as the purely political field

10   is concerned, I fully share Count Rechberg's regret at the diver-
gence of views, which has prevailed for years between the two
Cabinets on many important questions of domestic federal policy,
and I should welcome an understanding about them as in every-
body's interest. . . .

> Bismarck to Werther (Prussian Ambassador in Vienna), 28
> April 1863, (O. von Bismarck, *Gesammelte Werke*, vol iv,
> no. 79, p 114)

Questions

a Comment on Bismarck's belief that the entry of Austria into the
Zollverein was 'for both sides . . . unrealisable' (lines 2–3).
b How did Bismarck seek to soften the blow for Austria of not
being allowed into the *Zollverein*?
c To what extent does this extract amount to a repudiation of
Bismarck's words in document 5 above?

7 Draft treaty between Austria and Prussia in the wake of the war with Denmark, August 1864

1. The two Courts will watch in common that the question of
sovereignty in the duchies of Schleswig, Holstein and Lauenburg
shall not be brought to a hasty solution, but be kept open until
such time as the two Courts . . . consider it ripe for a definitive
5   decision. . . .
3. If, before the definitive arrangements over the duchies, complications should arise to disturb the state of possession of the Great
Powers, the Royal Prussian Court binds itself to [work together
with] the Imperial Austrian Court to the end that both the peace
10 treaty of Zurich shall be executed, and that Lombardy shall be
reunited with the Imperial state.
    The Imperial Austrian Court on its side, in the event of the
attainment of this aim, will renounce in favour of Prussia its share
of the rights to Schleswig, Holstein and Lauenburg which the
15 Crown of Denmark has ceded to Austria and Prussia jointly, and
will communicate its agreement to the union of these three duchies
to the Prussian monarchy.

> Ritter von Srbik (ed.) (1937) *Quellen zur Deutschen Politik
> österreichs*, Berlin, Oldenburg, no. 1768, p 271

Questions

a What was the 'hasty solution' (line 3) feared by Austria and
Prussia?
★ b What were the terms of the Treaty of Zurich?

c What does Clause 3 demonstrate about the territorial priorities of Austria?

8 The disintegration of the Third Germany

We have had another sitting of the Customs Conference today. Bavaria has now modified her motion, so that she is ready to join at once in deliberations with us on the tariff. Thus she has *given up* her insistence on preliminary negotiations with Austria.

5   In the same way, Württemberg, though making more fuss about it, has drawn even *closer* to our position.

Hesse-Cassel has quite come over *to our side*, accepts our tariff, accepts the French treaty, but wishes in connection with the latter, that we should make the attempt we have ourselves offered to
10 make in Paris, and has agreed that negotiations with Austria shall only take place after it. . . . Thus *Hesse-Cassel has separated herself from Hanover* – as her plenipotentiary tells me in confidence – because the Elector [of Hesse] has seen, from the last Hanoverian declaration, that Hanover thinks only of her [reward]. . . . From
15 now on the conferences will make progress. The current is favourable.

> Philippsborn (Director of Commercial Policy Section of the Prussian Foreign Office) to Bismarck, 29 February 1864, (*Die Auswärtige Politik Preussens*, vol v, no. 549, p 818)

Questions

a What was the essential purpose of the Customs Conference?
b 'Bavaria . . . has given up her insistence on preliminary negotiations with Austria' (lines 2–4). What was the political significance behind this?
c What was 'the French treaty' (line 8)?
d 'The current is favourable' (lines 15–16). What, specifically, was the writer alluding to, and why?

9 Bavaria bows to the inevitable

The course taken by the negotiations for the renewal of the *Zollverein* fills me with serious anxiety. From your reports, I have obtained corroboration of my view that Bavaria has no choice other than to form a Customs area of her own . . . or else to comply
5 with the Prussian demands for unconditional acceptance of the Franco–Prussian customs and commercial treaty.

However well-founded all the considerations . . . against the latter ... I yet believe we must decide for it. In her commercial policy Bavaria has been deserted by the other German states ... In my view, it is not obvious how far the consequent isolation of Bavaria and Württemberg can serve any useful purpose. The separation of their customs area from the rest of Germany is too unnatural for one to hope to build a tolerable, durable situation upon it. We should rather assume that the Government would sooner or later be forced ... to rejoin the rest of Germany. ... I believe that the Government would gain the support neither of Parliament nor of our business houses for a continuation of its present policy to the point of separation from the *Zollverein*. ...

I have asked myself whether it would not be advisable to begin negotiations with Prussia without delay. ...

> Louis II of Bavaria to Karl Schrenck, Bavarian Foreign Minister and Minister for Trade, 20 August 1864. (Munich, Hof-und-Staatsarchiv, Allgemeine Staatsarchiv, Ministerium des Handels, no 9693)

Questions

a 'In her commercial policy Bavaria has been deserted by the other German states' (lines 8–9). How true was this?

b Why did Louis II believe 'the Government would sooner or later be forced ... to rejoin the rest of Germany' (lines 14–15)?

c What was the Government of Bavaria's 'present policy' (line 18)?

d To what extent does this passage corroborate the views expressed in document 8 above?

10   Beating Prussia at her own game

(i) I must respectfully beg the favour of a decision as to Austria's further commercial policy at home and abroad. Prussia, in spite of her political relations with Austria, which are friendly, has deliberately continued to proceed in such a way as to make it impossible for the Imperial Government ever to realize the Customs Union, which by the treaty of February 1853 was set as Austria's and Prussia's common aim. Prussia has already significant results to show along this path. ... Despite its lack of reciprocity, the French commercial treaty has silenced all opposition in Prussia itself and, by its approach to the free trade system of the western powers, has clearly won power for itself in the Kingdom of Saxony and the Thuringian states, in Brunswick and Oldenburg. Moreover, the temper of the Parliaments in the medium-sized and southern states. In Bavaria, Württemberg, both Hessen, Nassau etc., have quite turned in favour of the treaty and the maintenance of the *Zollverein* despite it. It is only the governments in the last-named states and still more their princes personally who, for political reasons and in order to counteract the sole dominance of Prussia in economic matters, continue their opposition and seek support from Austria.

20 . . . Prussia does not owe these great successes only to her progressive industrialists and to their consciousness that they can stand up to competition from abroad. She owes them too to the consistency and single-minded direction with which the Berlin Cabinet, whether Liberal or Conservative statesmen hold the rudder, steadily uses the

25 implementation and extension of the *Zollverein* as the foundation and guideline for Prussian power in Germany and thoroughly exploits it against Austria. Finally the correctness of the economic principles, which have guided Prussian commercial policy, has very substantially contributed to her successes. It has been a policy of

30 breaking free from artificial assistance to protect particular branches of industry, and has favoured the free exchange of the products of the soil and of manufacturing industry in natural competition.

These principles . . . have latterly made further progress in Austria too. . . . Unfortunately the present Austrian draft tariff

35 appears, to most of the governments friendly to us, still insufficient in its lowering of duties and approach to the system of the Franco–Prussian commercial treaty. These governments desire a further considerable reduction of duties to make it possible for them and for us to prove to Prussia that no economic barrier lies in the way of

40 a German–Austrian Customs Union and that, therefore, only unjustifiable political motives dictate her wish at all costs to exclude Austria from participation in the *Zollverein* and from leadership of the economic interests of Germany.

Rechberg to the Emperor Franz Josef, May 1864. (Vienna Haus-Hof-und Staatsarchiv, Administrativ Regisratur F34 SR 3r8, Karton 40)

(ii) Our influence has sunk, not for the reason that we have

45 embarked upon this or that specific course, nor because we have fought for Denmark's integrity, nor because we are allied to Prussia, or have opposed the Liberal opinions of the day – for none of these reasons. We have lost reputation and sympathy just because we follow no specific policy. . . . We are seen to vacillate;

50 we are no longer feared; we are, therefore, less popular. Lasting popularity is never won by concessions to popular opinion. . . .

The medium-sized states will always come to us when they need, and they can only need us when we are powerful. They on their side afford us no support, as 1859 showed. We must now turn the

55 alliance with Prussia to good account . . . of course Prussia will always seek to drive us out of Germany; we can only fight Prussia if we combine with France and, since we do not wish to do that, our task is to prevent Prussia from falling into her arms. It will be easy

for us to counteract the disadvantageous results of the commercial
60 treaty with France if we decidedly turn to the system of free trade;
for the future belongs to it and we cannot escape it. We shall
also find it the most effective means of fusing England's interests
with ours. Moreover, England is neither an active ally nor a
decided enemy. ... In Germany it is time to cease to meddle and
65 muddle. ...

> Blome (Austrian Ambassador in Munich) to Alexander,
> Count von Mensdorff-Pouilly, newly appointed Austrian
> Foreign Minister, 29 October 1864. (Vienna, Haus-Hof-
> und Staatsarchiv, PA IV, no. 33)

Questions

a 'It is only the government ... who, for political reasons ...
   continue their opposition' (lines 16–19). Explain the nature of
   the political problem here.
b What evidence had Prussia given that she could 'stand up to
   competition from abroad' (lines 21–22)?
c How accurate is the assessment of Prussia's use of her economic
   strength given in the first extract?
d Who were 'most of the Governments friendly to us' (line 35).
e What inhibited Austria from offering a more sweeping lowering
   of duties?
f What are the 'concessions to popular opinion' referred to here?
   (line 51).
★ g 'Of course, Prussia will always seek to drive us out of Germany'
   (lines 55–56). Was this unduly cynical at this stage?
h To what extent do these two extracts show a continuity and
   coherence in Austrian policy-making?

11   A bitter reproach for Bismarck from the Austrian Chancellor

The ... question whether Austria will surrender the right to make a
Customs Union, and so acknowledge that, for commercial policy,
she does not belong to Germany, it is my duty as an Austrian
Minister to answer in the negative. What would one have said in
5 1815 to a proposal that essentially consisted in the exclusion of
Austria from a general German Customs and Trade association?
What would one have said to a stipulation that Austria should not
have any preference in trade and intercourse over the foreigner? If
we insist on our claim to a Customs Union, it is not because Prussia
10 has signed article 25 of the February treaty ... but rather that
because Austria is a German Power and cannot admit that a
common German institution should be completely closed to her

and that she should be treated as a foreign state by her fellow members in the Confederation.

> Rechberg to Bismarck, 17 September 1864, (*Die Auswärtige Politik Preussens*, vol v, no. 278, p 407)

Questions

a What is the significance of the reference to 1815?
b What was the February treaty (line 10)?
c Explain the nature of the *principle* outlined here by Rechberg. What possible answer might Bismarck have given to him?

12 The meaning of victory at Düppel

I am certainly no Bismarck enthusiast, but he has the ability to act. . . . I look forward to the future with pleasure. There is something invigorating, after 50 years of peace, in a day like the battle of Düppel for the young Prussian troops. One feels as if all one's
5 nerves had been refreshed. And what a blessing that in the face of all the manoeuvring of the princes and the grandiloquence of the true Germans the Austrian project for reform, and the *Nationalverein*, the full force of real power and real activism should make itself felt. . . . It is time that the importance of the medium–sized and
10 small states were kept within real limits. . . . They will go on saying that Prussia under Bismarck is not to be trusted; they will denounce more loudly than ever Prussia's greed for annexations and use it as a pretext for dissociating themselves; they will continue to say that the real Germany is outside Prussia and menaced by Prussia. . . .

> Letter from J. G. Droysen, a leader of the *Kleindeutsch* movement to W. Rossmann, 29 April 1864, quoted in W. M. Simon (ed.) (1968) *Germany in the Age of Bismarck* (Allen and Unwin)

Questions

★ a Who was Prussia fighting at the Battle of Düppel?
  b Explain the reference to 'all the manoeuverings of the princes' (line 6).

13 Weighing up the advantages and disadvantages of the Austrian alliance

(i) It will probably be possible to execute peacefully the minimum demand [competence separation of the duchies of Schleswig and Holstein from the Danish monarchy, both since 1864 provisionally

occupied by Austria and Prussia]. ... Open annexation ... will
5   probably lead to war against Austria. In this case France and Russia
would be likely to observe benevolent neutrality. War with Austria
sooner or later is probably anyhow not to be avoided; for Austria
has again adopted the policy of suppressing Prussia. ...

> Bismarck in meeting of Ministers, 29 May 1865, (*Die
> Auswärtige Politik Preussens* vol vi, no 101, p 179)

(ii) I think it more useful to continue for a while with the present
10 marriage despite small domestic quarrels, and if a divorce becomes
necessary, to take the prospects as they then prevail rather than to
cut the bond now, with all the disadvantages of obvious perfidy,
and without *now* having the *certainty* of finding better conditions in
a new relationship later.

> Bleichröder to Bismarck, 19 July 1865, quoted by Fritz
> Stern (1977) *Gold and Iron; Bismarck, Bleichröder and the
> building of the German Empire* (George Allen and Unwin)
> p 56

Questions

a   Why would France and Russia probably 'observe benevolent
neutrality' in a war between Austria and Prussia (line 6)?
b   Does Bismarck's tone suggest he was now resolved on war with
Prussia?
c   In what way had Austria 'again adopted the policy of suppressing Prussia' (line 8)?
d   What did Bleichröder mean by 'all the disadvantages of obvious
perfidy' (line 12)?
e   What reasons might Bleichröder have had for counselling
caution?

14   The Convention of Gastein, 14 August 1865

Article I. The exercise of the rights acquired in common by the
high contracting parties, in virtue of Article III of the Vienna
Treaty of Peace of 30 October 1864 shall, without prejudice to the
continuance of those rights of both Powers to the whole of both
5   duchies, pass to His Majesty the Emperor of Austria as regards the
Duchy of Holstein, and to His Majesty the King of Prussia as
regards the Duchy of Schleswig.
Article II. The high contracting parties will propose to the *Diet* the
establishment of a German fleet, and will fix upon the Harbour of
10 Kiel as a federal harbour for the said fleet. Until the resolutions of
the *Diet* with respect to this proposal have been carried into effect,
the ships of war of both Powers shall use this harbour, and the

command and the police duties within it shall be exercised by Prussia. ...

15 Article IV. While the division agreed upon in Article I of the present Convention continues, the Royal Prussian government shall retain two military roads through Holstein; the one from Lubeck to Kiel, the other from Hamburg to Rendsburg. ...

Article IX. His Majesty the Emperor of Austria cedes to His
20 Majesty the King of Prussia the rights acquired in the aforementioned Vienna Treaty of Peace with respect to the Duchy of Lauenburg; and in return the Royal Prussian Government binds itself to pay to the Austrian Government the sum of 2,500,000 Danish rixdolars. ...

25 Article X. ... The joint Command-in-Chief shall be dissolved on the complete evacuation of Holstein by the Prussian troops and of Schleswig by the Austrian troops, by the 15 September, at the latest. ...

Quoted by W. N. Medlicott and D. K. Coveney (eds)
(1971) Bismarck and Europe (Edward Arnold) pp 48–49

Questions

a   Suggest why Prussia was prepared to countenance the idea of a Federal Fleet at the port of Kiel?
b   What was the significance for Prussia of the acquisition of Lauenburg?
c   What grounds does this extract provide for doubting the durability of this settlement?

VI The End of the Confederation – War and Compromise: 1865–1867

The Convention of Gastein was designed to improve – even temporarily – Austro–Prussian relations. However, since Bismarck sought an assurance of Prussian autonomy north of the River Main, and since this was not forthcoming, it was clear almost at once it had only delayed a reckoning. Bismarck had also to contend with the growing anxiety of any *rapprochement* between France and Austria and he therefore contrived a meeting with Napoleon III in the summer of 1865 at Biarritz. The precise details of their meeting remain a matter of debate, although there is strong evidence that Bismarck encouraged Napoleon to formulate his territorial designs forthrightly and formally, arguably in order to be able to embarrass him at a later date. These included the detachment of Venetia from Austria, the Bavarian Rhineland as well as the Duchy of Luxembourg.

By the spring of 1866, plans for a war against Austria were already advanced in Berlin. This was only partly due to a confidence that, at this stage anyway, France would not intervene. Austria was inciting a strongly anti-Prussian sentiment in Holstein (much as Prussia provoked anti-Austrian feeling in Schleswig). In April, Bismarck secured an undertaking from Italy to go to war against Austria jointly, as long as hostilities erupted within three months. It is easy to overlook however that even at this juncture, Bismarck still kept alternative policies alive, encouraging the acceptance of a peace proposal made by the Gablenz brothers whereby Germany was to be divided into strictly Prussian and Autrian spheres of influence along the River Main. Austria was not at all enamoured of a plan which gave Prussia such entire ascendancy in northern Germany, and it quickly foundered, however.

Undoubtedly, it was Vienna's appeal to the Confederation to solve the duchies question – a blatant disregard for the provisions of the Gastein treaty – which provided Prussia with a *casus belli*, welcome to most of her leaders and unexpected as it was. Within a fortnight, Prussia had occupied Holstein and proclaimed a plan for a *Kleindeutschland*, robbing the Confederation of any good reason for remaining – and indeed Prussia declared its dissolution. But, while expanding skill and energy on the campaign ahead, Bismarck was alert to the risks. The Austrians had secured French neutrality in return for a promise to cede Venetia to Italy, and the huge majority of the Confederate states backed the Emperor.

In fact, the immense rapidity of Prussia's victory over the Austrians – Konnigratz was fought on 3 July – nullified most of these fears, though other problems arose. Bismarck had to propitiate Napoleon III, throwing out oblique hints that Rhineland or other territorial 'compensation' might be possible, while at the same time explain to a very reluctant King William (and very sceptical military leaders) that the diplomatic cost of gratifying their lust for further military conquest was unacceptable. Napoleon III, disgruntled and alarmed by events, was persuaded to act as mediator in the run up to the Preliminary Peace at Nikolausburg on 26 July 1866.

Austrian aspirations within Germany were annihilated by the scale of her defeat. Yet, except for Ventia, Bismarck succeeded in ensuring that she lost no territory. Her allies were dealt with less magnanimously: Hanover, Hesse-Kassel, Nassau and Frankfurt were all annexed by Prussia, which presided over the negotiations for the constitutional arrangements for the shape of 'Germany'. Now it was neither a single Confederation, nor an Empire. What was clear, however, was that the preoccupations (and to an extent the weaknesses) of other European statesmen had provided Bismarck with an opportunity which, with consummate skill, he had exploited. Henceforth, with a radically altered series of assumptions about the European power balance, the Great Powers would certainly be more vigilant. The need, therefore, for Bismarck to 'present' any future alterations to the *status quo* as compelling and unavoidable, was likely to be paramount.

1   Helplessness of the smaller German states before Prussia and Austria

If Austria and Prussia come to an understanding over a *provisorium* [provisional agreement] in Schleswig-Holstein that we regard as disadvantageous, can we come out against it?

    Only in the Press . . .

5   [If] Austria abandons Augustenburg what should we do?
(a) If the majority of the Confederation supports us, form a new Confederation of the medium-sized states with a Parliament.
(b) If only the minority supports us, protest and declare that we consider our task for the time being at an end.

10   This was agreed with Baron Beust, 12 August 1865.

> Note of Pfordten (Bavarian Prime Minister) on his meeting with Beust (Saxon Prime Minister), 12 August 1865, (Vienna, Haus-Hof-und Staatsarchiv, PA VI, no. 29)

a What did the writer believe could be accomplished 'in the Press' (line 4)?
b Explain the reference (line 5) to Augustenburg.
c Explain the option considered in lines 6–7.

2 The search for new allies for Prussia

During a conversation just held with the Italian envoy . . . I made the following suggestion:

That we should conclude a treaty of friendship, cast in general expressions of goodwill, in itself binding neither of the two Powers
5 to anything definite, but containing a promise to enter into negotiations for a specific war alliance as soon as one of the two Powers should consider that it had to conduct a war. In order that, in such a case, no further time should be lost in negotiations, the text of this second treaty should be agreed upon at the time of the
10 conclusion of the first. . . . Its signature should however be witheld and either Your Majesty's representative in Florence or the Italian envoy here be provided with such full powers that, on the outbreak of war, it would only be necessary for both governments to agree by telegraph on 'yes' or 'no'. . . .

> Bismarck to William I, 20 March 1866, (O. von Bismarck *Gesammelte Werke* vol v, p 412)

Questions

a Why did Bismarck suggest that, in the prospective treaty of friendship, specific terms should be enacted only in time of war?
b Why was Bismarck evidently anxious that 'no further time should be lost in negotiations' (line 8)?
c What would appear to have been Bismarck's underlying intentions in this treaty? Would these have necessarily been clear to the king at the time?

3 Divided Austrian counsels

[With regard to] . . . the threatening attitude, which Prussia has recently assumed in the Schleswig Holstein affair, His Majesty observed, raises the question whether we should calmly look on at these demonstrations or whether the honour, dignity and security
5 of Austria do not demand that such warlike preparations should be made as shall enable us calmly to face all eventualities. . . . On the other hand, one must probably take into serious consideration the

fact that the Prussian army was at present much more ready to take
the field and that the railway network there would greatly facilitate
10   its despatch to the chief strategic points, whereas our army had
been reduced to the utmost limit of an army on a peace footing. . . .

Count Mensdorff [said] . . . there was no occasion in the present
foreign relations of the Empire for an event so difficult to gauge in
its consequences as war; that, moreover, one could not tell where
15   fate could drive the government in Prussia, given the complications
of the internal situation there, the position of the government *vis à
vis* the Lower House. . . .

Count Esterházy [said] . . . we must show our teeth. It was the
task of our diplomacy so to define our attitude that our allies in the
20   Germanic Confederation could have no doubt at all about our
views and our conduct. . . .

The Finance Minister, Count Larisch, and the Minister of Trade,
Baron von Wüllerstorf, urged a peaceful solution . . . if events
should take a warlike turn, the repercussions upon the finances
25   and the economy . . . would have immeasurably disastrous consequences. . . .

His Majesty expressed, in conclusion, the opinion that . . . he
should leave warlike preparations for the time being aside and
should continue to seek the maintenance of the honour and dignity
30   . . . of the country by diplomatic means. . . .

> Meeting of Austrian Ministers with Emperor Franz Josef,
> 21 February 1866, quoted by Ritter von Srbik, (ed.) (1937)
> *Quellen zur deutschen Politik österreichs* (Berlin, Oldenburg)
> vol v, p 202

Questions

a   What was 'the threatening attitude which Prussia has recently
assumed' (lines 1–2)?
b   Explain the reference to the Prussian railway network (lines
9–10).
c   Paraphrase, in the simplest terms, Count Mensdorff's observations in lines 12–17.
★ d   Was Mensdorff right to lay stress on the troubled internal
situation in Prussia?
e   What 'diplomatic means' were open for Austria's purpose
(line 30)?

4   A war to suppress internal dissent?

So far . . . the differences between the two Powers [Austria and
Prussia] have been limited to the Cabinets. They have now been
transplanted to the field of public opinion. . . . I am clear that Count

Bismarck ... holds that the time has come to mount a great
5   Prussian action abroad and, if it can be done no other way, to
appeal to the arbitrament of war, and he thinks that circumstances
are favourable for this. Such an action has been from the beginning
the goal of his political career. It would suitably quiet his un-
governed and unscrupulous, but daring, thirst for achievement. ...
10   After such a success, especially if it were attained by means of a
fortunate war, the Government would more easily master the
internal strife. Its end without the diversion of war would be
subject to the most critical difficulties; for it is absolutely inconceiv-
able that King William could bring about legal recognition of the
15 principles represented by his Government without a *coup d'état*. His
Majesty is supposed to have positively refused his consent to the
coup d'état, which Count Bismarck may well have recommended.
The most effective, indeed the only means, of bringing about
a sudden change internally must thus be sought in the field of
20 foreign policy. It is such points of view which guide Bismarckian
policy. ...
How far Count Bismarck has succeeded, or will succeed, in
winning His Majesty for his extreme policy is precisely the
question on which the whole future depends ... a forcible solution
25 goes most decidedly against the grain with the king. Yet His
Majesty is easily accessible to personal influences and is especially
sensitive to illusions about supposed injuries to Prussian honour
etc. ...

> Károlyi (Austrian envoy in Berlin) to Count Mensdorff
> (new Austrian Foreign Minister), 22 February 1866,
> (Vienna, Haus-Hof-und Staatsarchiv, PA III, no. 91)

Questions

a   What is to be understood by 'public opinion' (line 3)?
b   'He thinks that the circumstances are favourable' (lines 6–7).
    Why might the writer have believed this?
c   What were the 'principles represented by his [King William's]
    Government' (line 15)? What evidence is there that these were
    presently causing such dissent?
d   Discuss the portrayal made here of the King of Prussia. To what
    extent is it corroborated by document 2?

5 Liberal opposition to the war of 1866

The victory of our arms [over Denmark] has restored our northern
boundaries to us. Such a victory would have elevated the national
spirit in every well-ordered state. But in Prussia, through the
disrespect shown for the rights of the reconquered provinces,

5 through the efforts of the Prussian government to annex them by
   force, and through the fatal jealousy of the two great powers, it has
   led to a conflict that reaches far beyond the original object of the
   dispute.

       We condemn the imminent war as a cabinet enterprise, serving
10 merely dynastic ends. It is unworthy of a civilised nation, threatens
   all achievements of 50 years of peace, and adds fuel to the greed of
   foreign countries.

       Princes and ministers who will be responsible for this unnatural
   war, or who increase its dangers for the sake of special interests,
15 will be guilty of a grave crime against the nation.

       The curse, and the punishment for high treason, shall strike those
   who will give up German territory in their negotiations with
   foreign powers.

                   Bebel (1911) *Reminiscences*, (New York: Socialist Literature
                   Company)

Questions

a In what way did victory over Denmark 'restore' Prussia's
   northern boundaries (line 1)?
b What was the 'disrespect shown for the rights of the reconquered provinces' (line 4)?
c What 'dynastic ends' was the 'imminent war' designed to serve
   (lines 9–10)?
d Explain the reference to German territory which risked being
   given up in negotiations with foreign powers (lines 17–18).

6 The fruits of an Austrian victory

(i) The material fruits of victory will of course be small, but it is the
moral gains from it we need. They will make amends for Magenta
and Solferino. . . . If, next, instead of a long peace a series of wars
were to follow, that too would have its good side: it would hold off
5 the revolution. . . . Without a war, there is only the prospect of
insecure peace or revolution. The perspective of further wars has,
therefore, little terror for me. Nor do I fear to pass for inhuman; for
revolution costs more streams of blood and undermines prosperity
more fundamentally than war and – which is often worse – it
10 destroys the moral strength of the nation which war, contrariwise,
raises. If we need war, but on the other hand ought not to attack,
we must oblige the enemy to attack by using means, which because
they remain strictly within the bounds of the law, cannot be made a
reproach to us. . . .
15   I had an audience today with old King Louis [of Bavaria] who
repeatedly called out: 'Now don't attack! Magnificent, the temper

in Austria! Congratulate the Emperor! Splendid! Quite different from Prussia ... But don't attack! ...'

> Blome (Austrian envoy in Munich) to Mensdorff, 20 May 1866 (Vienna, Haus-Hof-und Staatsarchiv, PA IV, no. 36)

(ii) God be praised and glorified! So we make progress in the
20 Holstein affair! ... Mistrust towards Austria will disappear, right thinking people will attain a majority in the Chamber and the governments will be strengthened in their opposition to Prussia. ... This declaration of ours ... must be published as soon as possible. Our interests demand it. Bismarck is unfortunately still
25 too weak to forge a cause of war from it. His position becomes more and more untenable every day owing to the cost of Prussian mobilisation. ... War, we need war, only war. The Congress is a humbug and a misfortune. ... Perhaps it may serve to let us see more clearly into Napoleon's intentions, but surely it will delay the
30 outbreak of war and spoil our position in Italy. ...

> Blome to Mensdorff, 29 May 1866 (Vienna, Haus-Hof- und Staatsarchiv, PA IV, no. 36)

Questions

a Discuss Blome's vision of 'moral gains' (line 2).
★ b Explain the reference to Magenta and Solferino (lines 2–3).
c What was the nature of the revolution anticipated by Blome?
d "But don't attack". Explain the rationale underlying the King of Bavaria's dictum.
e What was 'this declaration of ours' (line 23)?
f 'The Congress is humbug and a misfortune ...' (lines 27–28). Why so?
g Are these two extracts proof of political naïvete or are there signs of judgement and guile on the part of the author?

7 A warning to Hanover

It was the end of May and Miquel came from Hanover to Berlin to find out where he stood. ... Miquel insisted on a written invitation (as at that time it was considered a sin to go of one's own accord to Bismarck) and received one. ...

5 Bismarck: 'Now, how are things in Hanover? I have just concluded an alliance with your kingdom through Stockhausen.'

Miquel: 'Had you concluded 10 treaties with him, the King of Hanover would not go with you. ...'

Bismarck: '... We cannot do without Hanover. She has always

10   been on our side. . . . We cannot let Hanover, since it lies between
the two parts of our monarchy, stand against us. We must occupy
it if it votes against us in the Confederation.'

Miquel: 'Yes, but we cannot support you, if you break the
constitution like that?'

15   Bismarck: 'How otherwise can I deal with the King? Don't trouble
yourself now about the constitution. Later on, when we have won
our victory, you shall have your fill of constitutions. . . . I tell you,
we shall yet realise our aim, a short campaign in Bohemia, and we
shall checkmate the Austrians and the thing is done. It is your
20   national duty to stand by us.

Miquel: 'We should not go through with it.'

Bismarck: 'Then I tell you, we have not the least need of you. . . .'
Conversation of Bismarck with Miquel, 1866, (O. von
Bismarck *Gesammelte Werke*, vol vii, p 118)

Questions

a   Suggest why 'at that time, it was considered a sin to go of one's
own accord to Bismarck' (lines 3–4).
b   Explain Bismarck's statement: 'How otherwise can I deal with
the King?' (line 15).
c   '. . . you shall have your fill of constitutions' (line 17). What did
Bismarck imply by this? Assess the probable impact of this
statement upon its audience.
d   In what way might this passage be considered indicative of
Bismarck's style of manipulation and control?

8   'To the German people'

The Germanic confederation for half a century has represented and
promoted, not the unity, but the fragmentation of Germany. It has
long lost the confidence of the nation and for the foreigner counts
as a guarantee of Germany's continuing weakness. . . . Now, over
5   and above that, it has been abused in order to call Germany to arms
against one of its members: the very member who by its proposal
for the calling of a German Parliament had taken the first and
decisive step to satisfy the demand for national unity. . . .
    The decision of 14 June, when a majority of the members of the
10   Confederation passed a resolution to arm against Prussia, finally
violated the federal constitution and abolished the Confederation.
    All that remains is the basis of the Confederation: the living unity
of the German nation. It is the duty of governments and peoples to
find a new means of [constitutionally] expressing this. . . .

15   Prussia has the further duty ... of defending her independence, threatened by the decision of 14 June and the arming of her enemies. ... In doing so [Prussia] proclaims its decision to take up the struggle for the national unity of Germany hitherto thwarted by the self interest of individual states.

20   Immediately, on the dissolution of the Confederation, Prussia ... offered to the governments a new alliance based on the simple provision for mutual defence and participation in the national struggle. She sought nothing beyond the preservation of peace ... Prussia's offer has been declined. ...

25 When Prussia's troops cross her frontiers they do not come as enemies of the people. Prussia respects their independence and hopes to deliberate on the future destiny of our German fatherland together with their representatives in a German national assembly. ...

Quoted in H. Kohl (1888) *Dreisig Jahre preussich-deutscher Geschicte 1858–88 in amtlichen Kundgebungen* (Giessen) p 90

Questions

a What was the meaning of the claim that Prussia 'had taken the first and decisive step to satisfy the demand for national unity' (lines 7–8)?

b Why might Prussia's offer of a 'simple provision for mutual defence and participation in the national struggle' have been rejected (lines 21–23)?

★ *c* How fully were the hopes expressed in the last paragraph of this extract to be realised?

9   Perspective on Austrian defeat

Until today it has been impossible for me to recall the days that have just gone by partly for lack of time, but chiefly because I have been in too sad a mood to write down that I should like for ever to forget. On 3 July there took place ... the battle of Sadowa in which
5   eight Prussian Army corps gained a great victory, after a hard battle, over five Austrian army corps. The retreat soon degenerated into a mad flight so that the enemy gained an endless number of prisoners and 116 cannons, 70,000 men on both sides were killed, drowned in the Elbe, wounded or missing, or taken prisoner. In
10   short, Austria has perhaps never before suffered such a frightful defeat. In addition, a few days later she gave up Venice to France and entreated Napoleon to mediate for an armistice between herself, Italy and Prussia. ... Meanwhile, the Prussians advance in Bohemia and Moravia, meeting no resistance, for the northern
15   army seems completely broken up and dissolved ... it seems that irresponsible mistakes in leadership were once again committed

even if superior power and especially the terrible effect of the needle gun brought about the decision. Meanwhile there prevails in the Federal Army the most lamentable inactivity and confusion. ...

> Extract from the diary of the Baroness Spitzemberg, 8 July 1866, in R. Vierhaus (ed.) (1960) *Das Tagebuch der Baronin Spitzemberg*, (Göttingen) p 69 quoted in H. Böhme *op. cit.*

Questions

a Does the extract suggest that the Battle of Sadowa was a foregone conclusion?
b Comment on the scale of losses suffered by Austria in the war as described in this passage.
c What insights are given as to the reasons underlying the Austrian defeat?

10   Napoleon III counsels moderation

The Emperor [Napoleon III] answered me: Your urgent wish, then, is that the existence of the Imperial Austrian state should not be threatened. [He said] the destruction of Austria would cause a gap in the European state system, which could not be filled without
5 a general conflagaration. Russia would oppose her destruction. Nor might France be able to remain quiet. The war undertaken by Your Majesty was necessary to secure for Prussia a better position. It took courage that cannot be sufficiently admired for Your Majesty and Your Majesty's Minister President to undertake this war; for at
10 first the country was against it, and Europe no less so. Success must have exceeded Your Majesty's boldest hopes. ... He therefore advises Prussia not to go too far, to show moderation, and to be content with the consolidation of that position in the balance of power which she has justifiably won. ...

> Goltz (Prussian envoy in Paris) to William I, 4 July 1866 in H. Oncken, (1926) *Die Rheinpolitik Kaiser Napoleons III 1863–70*, vol i, p 301 quoted in H. Böhme *op. cit.*

Questions

a Why would Russia and France oppose the destruction of Austria (lines 1–5)?
b Comment on the nature of the 'courage' alluded to by Napoleon III (line 8).
c 'He ... advises Prussia not to go too far' (line 12). What precisely did Napoleon III want Prussia *not* to do?

11 The fruits of victory

(i) If hostilities are not continued – their continuation is unlikely – we have the prospect of the following peace terms: exclusion of Austria; the closest North German confederation under Prussia; its relations with South Germany reserved for free understanding; war
5   costs; the annexation of the duchies recognized, with a plebiscite in northern Schleswig; annexation of Hanover, Hesse-Cassel, Nassau, Upper Hesse and Frankfurt conceded by Austria and France . . . no land from Austria. There is no more to be had. Work so that our newspapers demand no more, but come out strongly for the
10 annexation of Hanover and Hesse.

> Bismarck to Count Fritz zu Eulenburg, Prussian Minister of the Interior. (O. von Bismarck *Gesammelte Werke*, vol vi, p 84)

(ii) On 23 July, under the presidency of the king, a council of war was held, in which the question to be decided was whether or not we should make peace under the conditions offered or continue the war. . . . I declared it to be my conviction that peace must be
15 concluded on the Austrian terms, but remained alone in my opinion; the king supported the military majority. . . . I was . . . overcome by a violent paroxysm of tears . . . and begged the king, in the event of his not accepting the advice for which I was responsible, to relieve me of my functions as minister if the war
20 were continued. . . .

We had to avoid wounding Austria too severely; we had to avoid leaving behind in her any unnecessary bitterness of feeling or desire for revenge; we ought rather to reserve the possibility of becoming friends again with our adversary of the moment, and in any case to
25 regard the Austrian state as a piece on the European chessboard and the renewal of friendly relations with her as a move open to us. If Austria were severely injured, she would become the ally of France and of every other opponent of ours; she would even sacrifice her anti-Russian interests for the sake of revenge on Prussia. . . .

> From Bismarck's *Memoirs* quoted in J. C. Rohl (ed.) (1970) *From Bismarck to Hitler: the problems of continuity in German History* (Longman) pp 20–21

30 (iii) Article I. With the exception of the Lombardo-Venetian Kingdom, the territory of the Austrian monarchy remains intact. . . . Article II. His Majesty the Emperor of Austria recognises the dissolution of the Germanic confederation as it has existed hitherto, and consents to a new organisation of Germany without the
35 participation of the Empire of Austria. His Majesty likewise promises to recognise the closer union which will be founded by His Majesty the King of Prussia, to the north of the line of the

Main, and he declares that he consents to the German states south
of that line entering into a union, the national relations of which
40   [will be formulated directly between themselves and the North
German confederation]. . . .
Article III. His Majesty the Emperor of Austria transfers to His
Majesty the King of Prussia all the rights . . . recognised as
belonging to him over the Duchies of Schleswig and Holstein, with
45   the reservation that the people of the northern districts of Schleswig
shall be again united to Denmark if they express a desire to be so by
a vote freely given.
Article IV. His Majesty the Emperor of Austria undertakes to pay
His Majesty the King of Prussia the sum of 40 000 000 *thaler* to
50   cover part of the expenses which Prussia has been put to by the
war. . . .
Article V. . . . the King of Prussia declares his readiness to let the
territorial state of the Kingdom of Saxony continue in its present
extent . . . reserving to himself . . . to regulate in detail the questions
55   as to Saxony's part in the expenses of the war, as well as the future
position of the Kingdom of Saxony in the North German confederation. . . .

> Preliminary Treaty of Peace between Austria and Prussia,
> 26 July 1866 in E. Hertslet (1875) *Map of Europe by Treaty*
> (London: vol iii, p 1698) quoted in H. Böhme *op. cit.*

Questions

a   'There is no more to be had' (line 8). What did Bismarck mean
by this?
b   Does the first extract here give any indication of public disquiet in
the wake of the war and, if so, of the form this disquiet might take?
c   Explain possible reasons for Bismarck's tears (line 17).
d   Is the highly emotional nature of the second extract fore-
shadowed by the tenor of the first passage?
e   Who might Bismarck have understood by 'our adversary of the
moment' (line 24)?
f   To what extent does the second extract betray concerned feeling
for the plight of Austria or naked *realpolitik*?
★ g   What was to happen to the Lombardo Venetian Kingdom (lines
30–31)?
h   What was the new organisation referred to in line 34?
i   Are there any major discrepancies between the provisions
outlined in the first extract and those attained in the third?

12   Austria baled out by smaller states

My dear husband . . . is very pleased with the peace concluded in
Berlin. . . . Württemberg is to pay 8 000 000 *gelder* in war indemnity

and, otherwise, is to remain with frontiers quite unaltered and unimpaired. There can be no question yet, on account of France, of
5 entry into the North German confederation. ... After peace had been concluded the King [of Prussia] made a very silly speech, that is, he scolded [our men] soundly for standing by Austria. In addition, Prussia has now annexed Hanover-Hesse-Cassel and Nassau. Baden is also to pay money. Bavaria seems likely to have
10 to surrender both land and money. Austria has gained a favourable peace at our cost. Prussia has been recommended to turn to us [the medium-sized states] for the damages she demanded in land and money and Austria esteems herself lucky to be rid of us. Since she gives up the cause, we too as a German state must give it up. ...

> Baroness Spitzemberg's diary, 19 August 1866 in R. Vierhaus (ed.) (1960) *Das Tagebuch der Baronin Spitzemberg* (Göttingen) p 72 quoted in H. Böhme *op. cit.*

Questions

a For whom could there be 'no question yet of entry into the North German confederation' (lines 4–5)? What interest had France in the matter?

b How reasonable was the idea that 'Austria had gained a favourable peace at our cost' (lines 10–11)?

★ c What was 'the cause' that Austria now gave up (line 14)? Did she adopt another in its place?

VII Bismarck as Mr Fixit
1867–69

Party identity – and especially the way in which parties in Prussia viewed Bismarck – were fundamentally altered by the successful prosecution of the Seven Weeks' War in 1866. Diehard Conservatives were perplexed, and quickly outraged, at his refusal to exploit Könnigratz by imposing a more authoritarian rule, while normal Liberal opposition found itself compromised by his readiness to conciliate. This was seen especially when he pushed ahead, despite the opposition of Cabinet and the reluctance of the king, with a bill, whereby the *Landtag* would indemnify the previous four years of government expenditure, authorised without their consent.

As Bismarck well knew, the Indemnity Bill provided the flashpoint for secessionist movements within both the major parties, resulting in the formation of a Free Conservative Party and of the National Liberals. Besides, surprising as it may have been that moderate Liberals ever agreed to vote for the Indemnity Bill, it seemed the only way at this time to keep the momentum for eventual unification.

Reconciliation of the parties contrasted sharply with the high-handed and cynical treatment of the annexed duchies. It was only mid-1867 that Bismarck permitted even moderate local autonomy to some of the annexed territories. His preoccupation was with the drafting of the constitution of the new North German confederation. It was agreed by Prussia and the other independent states north of the River Main to submit the draft of a constitution to a constituent assembly, voted by direct universal manhood suffrage, although the King of Prussia, as President of the new Confederation, would act as supreme commander of the armed forces.

The constitution itself is of especial importance to the historian: often seen as the product exclusively of Bismarck, it also shows that Bismarck himself was constrained by the political climate. The Presidency (*Praesidium*) headed the Confederation, assisted by the Federal Council (*Bundesrat*) and the Chamber of Deputies (*Reichstag*). In the *Bundesrat* sat representatives of the different member states within the Confederation, voting under mandate as in the old Federal *Diet* of 1815. Though Prussia had only 17 of a total of 43 seats, it would prove impossible to effect constitutional alteration without her consent, given that a two-thirds majority was necessary for such legislation. It also had a crisp executive function, possessing power of veto over unsatisfactory bills from the lower house (the *Reichstag*), without which it could not moreover be convened.

Creating a coherent role for the *Reichstag* betrayed the fundamental irreconcilability of Bismarck's aims. It had to be popular, serve as a theoretical constraint on the king and the administration, and yet he did not wish for parliamentary government. Universal male franchise was conceded, but deputies not paid, nor was there an annual budget, nor could Parliament dictate the level of military spending.

In the *Reichstag* elected in February 1867, the Conservatives won 59 seats out of a total 297, and the Free Conservatives 39, and the National Liberals 79. Faced with opposition over the draft constitution, Bismarck played off Liberal and Conservative fears, and granted minor concessions. What he would not agree to, to the chagrin of the National Liberals, was to make himself, as Chancellor, legally responsible to the *Reichstag*. Nor would he surrender critical Confederate expenditure – usually for military purposes – to annual parliamentary scrutiny and control. It took the Luxembourg crisis to persuade finally the Liberals to give way on this issue. In April 1867, the *Reichstag* ratified the constitution by 230 to 53.

The *political* strategy of the new Confederation was a good deal less certain. National Liberals and now the Free Conservatives urged the completion of unification and the weakness of the southern States was undoubted, but so too was the resolve of the French to oppose any incursions south of the Main. Bismarck, like Cavour in the build up to Garibaldi's landing in Sicily in 1860, would not commit himself to fewer than several quite alternative policies to prepare the way for an eventual unification.

The need to avoid provoking upset among the southern states was, perhaps, paramount for Bismarck. Napoleon's diplomatic manipulations over Luxembourg played into his hands to a considerable extent here. It had been garrisoned by Prussian troops since 1814, the King of Holland did not appear unwilling to sell it, and for Napoleon it represented a possibly fruitful 'compensation' after his disappointments in 1866 over his intended acquisition of the Palitinate. Napoleon's efforts to popularise the Luxembourg purchase were crude, and to some extent inflammatory. Certainly, notwithstanding Bismarck's earlier equivocation, the explosion of fury from the *Reichstag* in April 1867 over the Luxembourg initiative persuaded the Dutch to withdraw the offer to sell the duchy. Napoleon won a considerable concession in the London Conference that year, called to resolve the issue, when the Prussian garrison was ordered to be withdrawn, but the size of the diplomatic snub embittered him.

None of this, however, was nearly adequate to overcome southern particularism. The key states of southern Hesse and, above all, Bavaria were especially suspicious of Prussian intentions and it was in the face of Bavarian opposition that southern ministers agreed to a radical revision of the *Zollverein*. Bismarck had re-negotiated the terms of membership just after the Seven Weeks' War, but in the summer of 1867 he reminded the South that Prussia could dissolve it with just six months' notice.

The strategy here plainly was to pressure the South into a closer relationship through economic inducements – or sanctions. The elections for the new, democratically elected, customs union were therefore a bitter disappointment – and a highly unwelcome surprise – for Bismarck. He had probably overestimated the political influence of business in the South, markedly less industrialised than the northern states. The new customs union saw members of the north German *Reichstag* sitting alongside particularist, often Catholic, southern representatives, most of whom were strongly opposed to any political union with Prussia or the North German confederation. For the next two years, Bismarck seems to have accepted a gradualist approach to the question of German unity. Early in 1867, the southern states began a 'Prussianisation' of their forces, albeit unwillingly and slowly. Certainly, Bismarck in 1868 was warm in the support he gave Hohenlohe, Minister President of Bavaria, in his scheme for setting up a southern federation; subsequently, this was rejected by both Bavaria and Württemberg, but it had at least held out a means whereby southern particularism could be undermined.

1 Seeking an indemnity from the Prussian *Landtag*

The more sincerely the King's government desires peace, the more members of parliament feel it their duty to refrain from retrospective criticism, whether to defend or to attack. During the last four years members have spoken for their point of view repeatedly from
5   both sides, some with hostility, some with goodwill. During the last four years nobody on one side has been able to convince anybody on the other. Each has believed he was acting right as he did. The conclusion of peace in foreign relations, too, would be difficult to bring about if an acknowledgement were demanded
10 from one of the two contracting parties: 'I perceive now, that I have acted wrong'. We wish for peace in this domestic conflict, but not because we are not equal to the struggle. On the contrary, the tide is flowing more in our favour at this moment than it has done for years. Nor do we wish for peace in order to escape a possible
15 accusation under a law to be enacted in the future about responsibility. I do not believe we shall be accused. I do not believe that, if we are accused, we shall be condemned. ... We wish for peace because in our view the Fatherland needs it at the present moment

more than ever before. . . . We believe that we will find it because you
will have recognised that the King's government does not stand so far
from the aims which the majority of you also strive after, as you
perhaps have for years thought; nor so far as the silence of the
Government over much that had to be kept quiet could have justified
you in believing. . . . Thus we shall discharge the tasks, which remain
to be discharged, with you jointly. I in no way exclude from them
improvements of the domestic situation in fulfilment of the promises
given in the constitution. . . . But we can only discharge them
in common in so far as each side serves the same Fatherland with
the same goodwill without doubting the sincerity of the other. . . .

> Speech of Bismarck in the Prussian Lower House, 1
> September 1866 in H. Kohl (1915) *Bismarckreden 1847–95*,
> (Stuttgart) p 68 quoted in H. Böhme *op. cit.*

Questions

a   What did Bismarck imply by 'retrospective criticism' (line 2)?
b   Was it true that 'during the last four years nobody on one side
    has been able to convince anybody on the other'? (lines 6–7)?
c   Comment on 'the silence of the Government over much that
    had to be kept quiet' (lines 22–23).
d   What were the 'improvements in the domestic situation' (line
    26) which Bismarck had in mind?
★ e   For what *particular* actions was Bismarck seeking an indemnity?
★ f   Why was Bismarck confident that the *Landtag* might now be
    more receptive to his request for an indemnity?

2   Liberal climb down?

(i) The simple task of the next Parliament consists in rallying the
national elements . . . and in supporting the Government, according to our strength, in its efforts to set up a united and strong North
German state.
   What we have so far experienced in the course of negotiations
justifies our confidence that the constitution, to be laid before
Parliament before its enactment, truly expresses the nation's need
for unity and power. Members of parliament will, therefore, be in
the fortunate position of fighting by the side of the Government for
this aim for the first time since the awakening of German national
feeling. The time for ideals has passed. . . . Politicians today have to
ask less what is desirable than what is attainable. . . .

> Extract from a speech of J. Miquel (leader of the National
> Liberal Party in Prussia), December 1866 in W. Mommsen
> (1960) *Deutsche Parteiprogramme* (Munich) p 141 quoted in
> H. Böhme *op. cit.*

(ii) When the old Confederation broke up last year and the Prussian government announced its serious determination to . . . set
15 German unity on firmer foundations, we had no doubt that the Liberal forces of the nation would have to co-operate. . . . For this purpose we were ready for co-operation, but it would only be possible if the Government abandoned its violation of constitutional rights, acknowledged the principles so vigorously defended
20 by the Liberal Party, and asked for and obtained the indemnity. The groupings within the parties, shaped by the constitutional conflict, could not suffice to ensure this co-operation. The formation of the National Liberal, for the purpose of restoring the unity of Germany . . . met the new need. . . .

> Opening paragraph of the foundation programme of the National Liberal Party, June 1867 in W. Mommsen (1960) *Deutsche Parteiprogramme* (Munich) p 147

Questions

a '. . . the constitution . . . truly expresses the nation's need for unity and power' (lines 6–8). What gave the author this confidence?

b What did Miquel imply when he claimed that 'The time for ideals has passed' (line 11)?

c Why should the National Liberals have had 'no doubt that the Liberal forces of the nation would have to co-operate' (lines 15–16)?

d Comment on the Government's 'violation of constitutional rights' (lines 18–19).

e What was the National Liberal programme implying when it suggested that 'the groupings within the Parties . . . could not suffice to ensure this co-operation' (lines 20–22)?

3 Conservative schism

(i) The Conservative Party, without any change in its principles, seeks your firm support in loyal devotion to a king, who late in life went on to the battlefield for Germany's greatness and unity. . . . It will hold sacred the maxim it has received from its kings, that what
5 Prussia gains must be won for Germany. . . .

> From the Conservative Party *Reichstag* Party address for elections to the Prussian *Landtag*, 24 October 1867 (ibid) p 52

(ii) We set the *Fatherland always above the Party*; we put the *national interest above everything*.
The great task which was performed step by step in the creation

of the Prussian state, the *Zollverein*, and the North German
Confederation, goes now towards its fulfilment and completion:
not only in the inevitable union with the German South, but also in
the internal evolution of the new *German state* towards which, in
this *Reichstag*, the first significant steps have been taken. . . .

Even so, expressing the true Conservative spirit, we should
candidly and duly acknowledge the entry of this monarchy into the
ranks of the *constitutional states*. Absolutism has had its glorious past
in Prussia. Nowhere in the world has it left a more imperishable
memorial than this state, the work of complete royal power. But
the days of absolutism are over. . . .

We honour the state's contitution as a strengthening of the
kingdom, as a development of the nation, as a guarantee of the
freedom of the Church, and of the parity of denominations. . . . In
the same way we contest the out-of-date yet still propagated
doctrine of the separation of powers. . . .

We wish to support in manly independence the power of
Confederation and the government of the state, where its policy
agrees with our principles and especially where it puts *national
interest first*. . . .

> Election programme of the Free Conservative Party, 27
> October 1867 (*ibid*) p 54

Questions

a Why did the Conservative Party find it necessary (line 1) to
   stress that it was 'without any change in its principles'?
b 'What Prussia gains must be won for Germany' (lines 4–5).
   What implication lay behind this maxim?
c What did the authors understand by the 'internal evolution of
   the new German state' (line 12)?
★ d What consensus was there that the 'days of absolutism were
   over' (line 19)?
e Is there any significance in the stressing of the 'parity of
   denominations' (line 22)?
★ f Explain the 'doctrine of the separation of powers' (line 24).
★ g In what essential way did the programme of the Free Conservatives differ from that of the traditional group from whom it had
   now split?

4 The creation of the North German Confederation

(i) . . . the current drafts of the North German Constitution . . . too
much favour a centralised federal state for the future accession of
the South Germans. In form, it will have to incline more to a league

of states. It can be given the character, in practice, of a federal state
by means of elastic turns of phrase apparently meaningless but in
fact having wide implications. ...

We must make over to the central institutions the subjects on
which they have power to legislate as soon as possible. We adhere
to the programme, announced before the war, that federal laws
shall be enacted by agreement of the majority of the Federal *Diet*
with that of the representative assembly.

In my view, the essentials are: no assembly of estates, no [system
of indirect voting] and no property qualifications for the vote. ...

Memorandum of Bismarck, 30 October 1866 (O. von
Bismarck *Gesammelte Werke* vol vi, no. 615, p 167)

(ii) The plan of a federation now before us ... is in no way a
constitutional monarchy, nor is it a federation according to traditional theories which have been developed in our universities. ...

Those who have drawn up the plan have ... pursued a path
exactly opposite to that which has hitherto been followed in
Germany ... they have sought out the really existing forces in the
long chaos of German conditions; they have sought to give them a
legal basis, as well as a form adjusted to the power and importance
of each. ...

The forces to be considered, as everyone here knows well, were
the powerful, triumphant Prussia. ... It is quite necessary that she
wield dictatorial power, considering the situation in Europe at the
present time. On the other hand, there are other German states
which, in the struggle against Prussia, by no means won any
laurels. Even those who were her allies were cast into the shade by
the tremendous increase in Prussia's power. Yet, despite their
relation with Prussia, the various German states have shown a
marked vitality and, on occasion, enjoy a strong support from the
outside. In addition, and this has weighed most heavily, despite the
efforts of the cultivated class toward unification, the individual
states retain the real sympathy of their own people.

Last, there was a liberal public opinion – in Prussia, in Germany,
in Europe. In Prussia, it appeared that public opinion had been
defeated in the unsuccessful opposition to the ministry of Bismarck. ... Yet, despite all this, in the entire range of European
relations, this same public opinion has grown stronger and stronger,
until not even the most powerful of military monarchies can for all
time resist the spirit of public opinion.

It was necessary, then, to consider these three forces: (1) the
military demands of the great Prussian state; (2) the demands of the
various individual states, which were supported by local sentiment;
and (3) the strength of public opinion. The draft of the Constitution
... provides for an organ for each of these forces: to Prussia, to the
Crown of Prussia – is assigned the presidency of the federation; to

the smaller states – the *Bundesrat* [representing the princes]; to public opinion, the *Reichstag* [representing the public].

> Extracts from a speech by the historian Heinrich von Sybel before the Constituent Assembly, 1867, quoted in L. L. Snyder (ed.) (1958) *Documents on German History* (Rutgers University Press)

50 (iii) The more we penetrate into the intricacies of the North German Constitution, the more we become convinced that its whole framework is built up with reference to the exceptional and extraordinary position of the Chancellor ... and to the concentration into his own hands of the vast administrative power vested in
55 the Federal Chancellor's department. ... The government of North Germany is tending daily to become as much a personal government as that of France. ... No man can be a *bona fide* leader of a great Liberal party without faith in Liberal principles, and not
60 one mustard seed of such faith exists in Count Bismarck's nature.

> Sir Richard Morier to Lord Stanley, 1868, quoted in C. Grant Robertson (1969) *Bismarck* (New York)

Questions

  a Why was it necessary for the North German Constitution 'in form ... to incline more to a league of states' (lines 3–4)?

★ *b* Explain how federal laws were to be passed (lines 9–10). Did this amount to a true compromise between national and particularist feeling?

★ *c* Why was Bismarck so keen to have universal, equal and secret suffrage?

  d What is to be understood by the observation (lines 30–31) that 'the various German states have shown a marked vitality'? What support did they 'enjoy from the outside'?

  e Comment on what is to be understood by 'public opinion' in the second extract? What warning was contained for the government therein?

★ *f* How accurately has the author in the second passage interpreted the intentions of Bismarck?

  g '... the exceptional and extraordinary position of the chancellor' (lines 52–53). Is this in any way hinted at in either of the first two passages?

  h What is meant by the reference to Prussia becoming 'as much a personal government as that of France' (lines 56–57)?

5   International repercussions

(i) However great the value that we attach to our relations with France, we cannot afford to be beguiled into compromising ourselves by any initiative which would shake our whole position in Germany to the deepest point. The French alliance, if bought by a humiliating outrage upon German national feeling, is bought too dear. ... Alliance with France is in an eminent degree advantageous, but it is not the only aim of Prussian policy nor an *overriding* one. ... You should rather hold back a decision by playing for time until events make it *easier* or unnecessary. ...

> Bismarck to Goltz (Prussian Ambassador in Paris), 13 January 1867, in H. Oncken, *Die Rheinpolitik Kaiser Napoleons III 1863–70*, vol ii, no. 335, p 180 quoted in H. Böhme *op. cit.*

(ii) In the press, as in the public at large, the question is actively discussed: what attitude would Austria have to take on the occurrence [of a conflict between Prussia and France]. ... I should like to draw special attention to three currents of opinion.

The first one is decidedly hostile to Prussia. The supporters of this opinion, though they form a numerical minority, belong to the higher and privileged ranks of society and exercise ... an influence that is not to be disparaged. ... They breathe only detestation and revenge against Prussia and look with bitter dislike upon the successes of Prussian policy. ...

A second and third current of public opinion ... have the common characteristic that they consider the maintenance of peace as a prerequisite for the success of Austria's constitutional reconstruction and both agree that an alliance with France, whatever the circumstances, would be very horrifying. ...

A large party in Austria cherished the hope after the war, and still may well yield to it, that a parliamentary life in the western half of the Austrian empire, developed on broad liberal principles, might exercise a strong attraction upon the south German states and form a bridge to a closer league between them and German Austria. ...

The course of events, the existing organisation of the relations of Prussia to the South German states ... have since destroyed some of these illusions. The untiring efforts of a great number of Austrian newspapers bear witness, however, that they survive on many sides. These efforts are directed to throwing suspicion on Prussia's German policy, to drawing attention to the alleged reactionary tendencies of the constitution of the North German Confederation and to attacking the new situation in the states annexed to Prussia in the most spiteful and slanderous way ...

This party ... speculates about the political conjectures which might force Prussia to make concessions in this connection to Austria. A warlike entanglement of Prussia with France is considered such a conjecture. ...

Finally, a third current of opinion openly declares that the formation of a South German Confederation is, after the events of

45   last year, no longer possible. I should designate this as the direction of opinion most widely supported and especially prevalent among the bourgeoisie. They acknowledge that . . . a surrender of South Germany to Austria would be as good as requiring Prussia to give up something she had already won; and they are under no illusions
50   that Prussia, despite all the dangers threatening from France, will ever willingly agree to that. . . .

    The supporters of this policy wish for co-operation with Germany, after it has been united under Prussia's leadership . . . they aim here at a . . . political alliance based on similar economic
55   interests. The advantages of such an alliance would have to be sought by Austria less in Germany than in the Near East. . . .

            Landenberg (Prussian Envoy in Austria) to Bismarck, 2 September 1867 (Bonn, Auswärtiges Amt, IAA, no. 54, vol iv)

    (iii) Baron Beust [the Austrian Foreign Minister] said [to me] . . . the notion now prevailed in France that Prussia wished to absorb South Germany. This notion disquietened public opinion and
60   would lead to war unless it was removed. The French could only be quieted by the foundation of a South German League . . .

            Note by Hohenloe, (Minister President of Bavaria) 6 November 1867. (*Die Auswärtige Politik Preussens*) vol ix, no. 295, p 361)

Questions

   a   What kind of situation did Bismarck envisage when he wrote of 'compromising ourselves' (lines 2–3)?

★ *b*   In what ways was an alliance with France 'in an eminent degree advantageous' (line 6)?

   c   '. . . both agree an alliance with France . . . would be very horrifying' (lines 23–24). Explain this thinking. Was such news encouraging for Bismarck?

   d   What 'illusions' had 'the existing organization of the relations of Prussia to the South German states . . . destroyed' (lines 30–32)?

★ *e*   How did the author of the second passage imply Bismarck was to woo 'the third current of opinion' he identiified (line 43)? Were the hopes he outlined here as belonging to this third group to be realised?

★ *f*   To what extent do the feelings in the third passage contradict or reinforce those outlined in the previous two?

   g   How plausible an idea at this time was 'the foundation of a South German League' (line 44)? Which state would be expected to lead it?

6 The dilemma of the South German states

(i) Count Bismarck told me yesterday . . . that . . . he was enacting a constitution from which, he hoped, a far better relationship to us and to the south than that in the Confederation [of 1815] would arise.

5   It would leave the individual states the greatest administrative freedom, but the entire military power [of Germany] would pass into the hands of Prussia. . . .

> Wimpffen (Austrian envoy in Berlin) to Beust, 16 December 1866. (*Die Auswärtige Politik Preussens*, vol viii, no. 136, p 213)

(ii) The reception which Prince Hohenlohe gave me . . . shows unmistakably his wish to cultivate good relations with the Austrian
10   representative. . . . I do not overlook the fact that his leaning towards Prussia is just as unmistakable. . . . But Bavaria, both in the person of its king and in the feeling of its population is very jealous of its undiminished sovereign rights. . . .

      . . . [Hohenlohe is] prevented from giving friendship with
15   Prussia too firm and binding a form in the first place by the well-founded jealousy of the king for his complete and free sovereignty . . . and in the second place, by uncertainty whether there would be a parliamentary majority in favour of such a course. . . .

> Trauttmansdorf (Austrian envoy in Munich) to Beust, 24 January 1867. (Vienna, Haus-hof-und Staatsarchiv, PA IV, no. 36)

(iii) I cannot indeed conceal from you the fact that the majority of
20   the south German people, the real mass of the people, is obviously unfavourable to any closer connection with Prussia . . . through too close a tie injury could be done to our institutions, to our independence . . . the South German stocks have always been attached with great constancy to their institutions . . . the mass of
25   the people, among us just as everywhere, engages in the politics of emotions only.

> Wolfgang von Thüngen, Bavarian politician in 1867, to an assembly representing the states of the *Zollverein* quoted in H. Böhme *op. cit.*

Questions

a   What was the significance of leaving the individual states 'the greatest administrative freedom' (lines 5–6)?

★   b   What picture of Bavarian policy emerges from the second passage? Why were there clear signs of equivocation?

c   'the mass of the people . . . engages in the politics of emotions only' (lines 25–26). Is that the situation depicted by the first two passages as well?

★   *d*   In what ways might von Thüngen's words have been especially tailored to suit this particular audience?

7   Prussian perspectives on Bavaria

(i) ... we keep the aim [of unification] steadily before us ... we have to watch each time we negotiate a new step forward that we do not endanger what has already been achieved. ...

5   The danger lies before us that too quick an advance might drive Bavaria, with its strong Ultramontane and Particularist elements, into the enemy's camp. ... The Customs Parliament meets in a little while. We consider ourselves bound to wait to see what temper this assembly shows. We find ourselves justified in hoping that it will be inclined to prepare the extension to the South

10   German states ... of the laws which have been already enacted for the North German Confederation ... namely those on citizenship, passports and civil procedure. ...

> Bismarck to Flemming (Prussian Envoy in Karlsruhe), 3 December 1867, (O. von Bismarck, *Gesammelte Werke*, vol vi a, no. 974, p 154)

(ii) ... we regard with satisfaction Prince Hohenlohe's efforts to bring about the reform of the armies in the South German states in

15   common, so that they may approximate as much as possible in organisation to that of Prussia. ...

We stand towards the South German states in a different, one might say more favourable, relationship than towards the North German ones. Our own security demands that the bonds between

20   us and the North German states should be drawn as tight as possible within the federal situation, and that we should have the unconditional disposition of the domestic and foreign forces of the North German Confederation. ... In regard to South Germany, we do not need the same strict form of union. We need only such

25   an unambiguous expression of national community of interests as will give us confidence that the South German states will never be tempted into a hostile attitude towards North Germany or into reliance upon foreign Powers and that regard for the common economic interests of the German people will always be assured by

30   common organic institutions. ...

> Bismark to Reuss (Prussian envoy in Munich), 22 January 1867, (O. von Bismarck, *Gesammelte Werke*, vol vi, no. 663, p 240)

    a Comment on 'the strong Ultramontane and Particularist elements in Bavaria' (line 5).

★   *b* Why should Bismarck be writing this to the Prussian envoy in Württemberg?

★   *c* 'In regard to South Germany, we do not need the same strict form of union' (lines 23–24). Was this an accurate representation of Bismarck's feelings at this time?

    d Why did Bismark take good care to stress in this passage the 'common economic interests' and 'common organic institutions of the German people' (lines 28–30)?

8 The economic dimensions of unification

(i) Besides working to found the North German Confederation, the Government is striving for the association of this national federation with the South. ... Two kinds of circumstance will naturally exercise an overwhelming influence in the question of the
5 establishment of such a wider league: the economic and the military ... here the opinion prevails that the South gets more out of [the *Zollverein*] than the North and, therefore, the *Zollverein* should be limited to the North. Moreover, the six months' notice hangs over the heads of the South German industrialists and traders like a
10 sword of Damocles. The continuation of the *Zollverein* and the alteration of its precarious duration into a firm term of so many years is, however, acknowledged to be in the interest of the south ... this will be looked on as a concession which ... must be answered with a counter-concession. The South can provide this
15 counter-concession in the military field. Berlin has its attention firmly fixed on the possibility of attack from France, allied with Austria. The alliance of South with North Germany would be of priceless value for such an event. ... The conclusion ... is that Prussia will not let herself be disturbed in her work for the North
20 German Confederation by the attitude of the South, but that it can cause her to promote the formation of a wider international league consisting of North Germany on one side and the southern states on the other. In this alliance the South will attain the more in the economic field, the more it is in a position to offer in the military
25 field. ....

        Spitzemberg (Berlin) to Varnbühler (Minister President of Württemberg), 26 January 1867, (*Die Auswärtige Politik Preussens*), vol viii, no. 207, p 332)

(ii) ... Württemberg, Baden and Hesse are ready to negotiate with the North German Confederation. ... The economic interests of

Bavaria are linked in such manifold ways with those of the rest of Germany that she could not let the links be cut. ... The king's Government cannot, therefore, exclude itself from negotiations with the North German Confederation. ...

> Circular despatch of Hohenlohe, 30 April 1867 in F. Curtis (ed.) (1906) *Denwürdigkeiten des Fürsten Chlodwig Hohenloe-Schillingfürst* (Leipzig) vol i, p 243

Questions

a Why should it be that 'here the opinion prevails that the South gets more out of the *Zollverein* than the North' (lines 6–7)?

b What was 'the six months notice hanging over the heads of the German industrialists' (lines 8–9)?

c Explain the nature of the 'counter-concession' (line 14) Prussia sought from the south.

d What is meant by 'Prussia will not let herself be disturbed in her work for the North German Confederation by the attitude of the South' (lines 19–20)?

★ *e* How great were the possibilities of an attack from France at this point?

f Why could 'Bavaria ... not let the links be cut' (line 29).

★ *g* Why is there a tone of apparent reluctance in the second passage? Was this reluctance merely contrived for his audience?

9 Elections to the German Customs Parliament

(i) ... that course seems to be most beneficial which will most quickly lead the South German states voluntarily into the North German Confederation. ... Everything turns upon the direction in which public opinion in South Germany evolves and the speed with which it does so ... the next task is [therefore] to work for the speedy summoning of the Customs Parliament and to encourage, or to awaken, the demand for the extension of the scope of its jurisdiction and for drawing to it new subjects of discussion. ...

> Bismarck to Flemming (Prussian envoy in Karlsruhe), 13 November 1867, (O. von Bismarck, *Gesammelte Werke*, vol vi a, no. 934, p 113)

(ii) ... the Liberal Party is developing all its strength in order to prepare for entry into the North German Confederation through the elections to the Customs Parliament. The Government and the great mass of the population stand perplexed and discouraged between the two extremes. This beautiful land drives rudderless towards an uncertain future and whether her fate is hurried forward

15   or delayed only depends on whether or not a war with France lies
ahead. . . .

> Werthen (Prussian envoy in Munich) to Bismarck, 20
> January 1868. (*Die Auswärtige Politik Preussen*, vol ix, no.
> 521, p 626)

(iii) Today the *Neuesten Nachrichten* gives the results of the elections
as follows: Liberals: 14 sure, 6 expected; Centre: 9 . . . Ultramontanes: 20 . . . .

20   The Ultramontanes have thus won a brilliant victory . . . By and
large, the victory is very astonishing. It stands in direct contrast to
the majority in the Lower House and affords proof that the great
mass of the people are still quite incapable of thinking for themselves and are in the hands of a secret, powerful party, whose roots

25   lie outside the country. This . . . will not fail to have repercussions
among the intelligent section of the population . . .

> Werthen to Bismarck, 15 February 1868, (Ibid, vol ix, no.
> 596, p 704)

(iv) 'The protest of South Germany against Prussification' – we
must certainly so characterise the outcome of the elections to the
Customs Parliament. . . . It is as well deserved a censure as ever any

30   was. . . .

   . . . *What attitude will the Governments take towards the German
protest of the population?* . . . In Baden the answer to the country has
been the nomination of a Prussian Minister of War. Here in
Württemberg something similar is said to be contemplated. . . .

35   *If only south Germany had a statesman*, just a single one who had
confidence in himself, confidence in the people and the confidence
of the people! . . . The German *Volkpartei* itself must be the saviour.
It must turn the German protest of our people against Prussification
into organisation and action against Prussification. . . .

> Extract from a Swabian popular newspaper, 8 March 1868,
> (*Der Beobachter*, 38, no. 57, p 1)

Questions

a   What is there about the first passage that denotes a hint of
    urgency?
b   Explain what should be understood by 'public opinion' in the
    first passage?
c   What 'new subjects of discussion' (line 8) did Bismarck wish to
    draw to the Customs Parliament?
d   Why were the Bavarian Government and the masses 'discour-
    aged and perplexed' (line 12)?
e   Why does the author of the second passage attribute such
    significance to the possibility of a war with France (lines 15–16)?

f Was there any 'secret, powerful party whose roots lie outside the country' (lines 24–25)? What 'repercussions' was he referring to (line 25)?

g Discuss the analysis of the election results put forward in the third passage. Is it corroborated or refuted by the tenor and arguments put forward in the final extract?

★ *h* Who were the German *Volkspartei*?

★ *i* What is to be understood here by 'Prussification'?

VIII War against France and the southern states subdued – 1870

Germany became unified because the southern states feared that, if they did not acede to the wishes of Prussia, they risked being overrun in the course of the Franco–Prussian war. The war happened because of a major diplomatic confrontation, the origins of which lay in Bismarck's efforts to secure for Prince Leopold of Hohenzollern the vacant Spanish throne.

The historiography of this episode is contentious, although there is widespread agreement that Bismarck was, at least, prepared to risk war with France as a result of promoting his candidate. King William was dubious from the first, and Prince Leopold himself had great distaste for the idea. Considerable pressure was brought to bear upon him by Bismarck until he agreed to allow his name to be put forward in June. A Prussian clerical error delayed the quick ratification for which Bismarck had looked from the Spanish *Cortes* to pre-empt the French fury which he knew must result. The news broke in Paris before the Spanish had decided, and in a state of some anxiety the King of Prussia persuaded Prince Leopold to cancel his candidature.

Bismarck's prestige might never have survived this but for sheer chance: Gramont, the irascible new French foreign minister, provocatively demanded a guarantee that the candidacy would not be refused, and instructed the French ambassador in Berlin, Count Benedetti, to seek an audience with the King to that end. This the King, incensed by such a snub, refused to do. His account of the episode was transmitted to Bismarck in the Ems telegram, who altered it in such a way as to stress the peremptory treatment of Benedetti by the King. Bellicose opinion in France was inflamed to the point where Napoleon III felt constrained to declare war on 15 July.

Bismarck's editing has often been blamed as the action which provoked the French into a declaration of war – and one which was designed to do as such. Certainly he encouraged this belief in his garrulous reminiscences. Yet the refusal to grant the ambassador an audience was the king's decision, and Bismarck did not alter the substance of the telegram. Nonetheless, there was no disguising the preparedness and high morale of the Prussian forces in the war. Austria refused to assist France without Italian help, and the Italians in 1869 had made French withdrawal of their garrison in Rome a *sine qua non* of any assistance in a war on the side of the French. Britain had been outraged by Bismarck's carefully leaked negotiations over Belgium and mollified by Prussia's promises to respect Belgian neutrality. Russia, shortly after the French defeat at Sedan in September, took advantage of the diplomatic confusion to repudiate the Black Sea clauses imposed on her by the Treaty of Paris.

This latter incident was merely the most conspicuous of several which pointed towards an internationalisation of the conflict. Bismarck was understandably anxious to defuse any wider unrest. He knew that unification rested firstly on an explosion of nationalist feeling in the south and, secondly, the hard-headed recognition of Bavaria and Württemberg that, in the wake of the war, they were too vulnerable to stay outside any putative Germany. Bismarck worked hard to effect a rapid constitutional recognition of their quiescence, conceding more in the way of federal autonomy than he might have wished, especially in Bavaria and Württemberg, although Prussia still exercised *de facto* control over the *Bundesrat*.

The military, and most especially von Moltke, sought a far more vengeful victory over France than Bismarck would countenance, and he successfully wrested from Moltke the king's authority to negotiate an armistice. The greatest – and unexpected – difficulties Bismarck experienced however were with his own king, whose appreciation of Bismarck's qualities were severely shaken by the nature of the victory with which Bismarck presented him. It took the tactful persuasion of King Louis of Bavaria and all the firm determination of the Chancellor to persuade a reluctant and violently resentful King William that he must become the German Emperor.

It was on 18 January 1871 that the German Empire was proclaimed in the Hall of Mirrors at Versailles. It took until May for the Treaty of Frankfurt finally to confirm peace between France and Prussia. The loss of Alsace and much of Lorraine, the imposition of a heavy indemnity and the presence of an army of occupation suggest that Bismarck's vaunted 'leniency' had either subsided of its own accord or in the face of pressure from conservative *élites* within the new Germany.

Europe could not but recognise that something critical had changed. Less significant, perhaps, than the territorial adjustments were the violent resentments of the French and the anxiety of Germany, as it sought – still under the aegis of Bismarck – to isolate an enemy it believed it now could never appease.

1 Bismarck predicts war

(i) Unhappily, I believe in a war with France before long – her vanity, hurt by our victories, will drive her in that direction. Yet, since I do not know of any French or German interests requiring a

resort to arms, I do not see it as certain. Only a country's most vital
interests justify embarking on war – only its honour, which is not
to be confused with so-called prestige. No statesman has a right to
begin a war simply because, in his opinion, it is inevitable in a given
period of time. If foreign ministers had followed their rulers and
military commanders into the field, history would record fewer
wars. On the battlefield – and, what is far worse, in the hospitals – I
have seen the flower of our youth struck down by wounds and
disease. From the window, I can see many a cripple hobbling along
the Wilhelmstrasse, looking up and thinking to himself that if the
men up there had not made that wicked war I would be at home
strong and well. Such memories and sights would leave me
without a moment's peace if I thought I had made the war from
personal ambition or national vanity. . . . You may rest assured that
I shall never advise His Majesty to wage war unless the most vital
interests of the Fatherland require it.

> Bismarck to Count Bethusy-Huc (Conservative Deputy in
> the *Landtag*), March 1867, quoted by A. Palmer (1976) in
> *Bismarck* (Charles Scribner's Sons) p 133

(ii) . . . I also think it probable that German unity will be forwarded
through violent events. It is quite another matter, however, to
bring about such a catastrophe and to bear responsibility for the
choice of the time for it . . . German unity is not at this moment a
ripe fruit. . . . The capacity to wait while circumstances develop is
one of the prerequisites of a practical policy . . .

> Bismarck to Werthen (Prussian envoy in Munich), 26
> February 1869, (O. von Bismarck *Gesammelte Werke*, vol
> vi b, no. 1327, p 2)

(iii) In regard to the South German situation, I think the line for
Prussian policy is set by two diverse aims. . . . The distant and
greater aim is the national unification of Germany. . . . We cannot
accelerate it unless out-of-the-way events in Europe, such as some
upheaval in France or a war of other Great Powers among
themselves offer us an unsought opportunity to do so. . . . I
consider [our immediate] aim to be to keep, first, the Bavarian
government and, secondly, the Württemberg government in such a
political direction that as long as the *status quo* lasts, neither Cabinet
will co-operate with Paris or Vienna, not . . . to loosen or even to
break the alliances which have been concluded. . . .

> Bismarck to William I, 20 November 1869 (Ibid, p 162)

Questions

a   'I do not know of any French or German interests requiring a
resort to arms . . .' (lines 3–4). How truthful was this?

b   Comment on Bismarck's distinction between 'prestige' and 'honour' (lines 5–6).
c   'The most vital interests of the Fatherland' (lines 18–19). What might these comprise?
d   What reasons might Bismarck have for his apparently reasonable and modest disclaimer of warmongering in the first extract?
e   In what ways does the second extract show a markedly different attitude to the possibility of war?
★ f   How might this different attitude be explained by the unfolding of European politics between 1867 and 1869?
g   Comment on Bismarck's assertion in the third extract that 'The distant and greater aim is the national unification of Germany' (lines 26–27).
★ h   Explain Bismarck's concern over the political direction of Bavaria and Württemberg.
i   What were 'the alliances which have [just] been concluded' (line 35)?
★ j   What are the reasons to doubt the absolute truthfulness of any one of these sources?

2   The Hohenzollern candidature

(i) . . . I am of the opinion that it would serve Prussian and German state interests. . . . The Spaniards would have a feeling of gratitude towards Germany, if they are rescued from the state of anarchy into which a people predominantly monarchist in sentiment threatens to
5   sink because it lacks a king.

For Germany it is desirable to have on the other side of France a country on whose sympathies we can rely and with whose feelings France is obliged to reckon . . . French peaceableness towards Germany will always wax or wane in proportion to the dangers of
10   war with Germany. We have in the long run to look for the preservation of peace not to the goodwill of France but to the impression created by our position of strength.

. . . It is therefore to Germany's political interest that the House of Hohenzollern should gain an esteem and an exalted position in
15   the world such as does not find its analogy in the past record of the Habsburgs since Charles V. . . . Just as in Spain scant respect for the ruling house has paralysed the forces of the nation for centuries, so with us pride in an illustrious dynasty has been a powerful moral impetus to the development of Prussia's power in Germany. . . .
20   A rejection of the proferred crown would probably have undesirable consequences. It could not but highly offend the Spaniards. . . .

Bismarck to the King of Prussia, 9 March 1870 in Georges Bonnin (ed.) 'Bismarck and the Hohenzollern Candidature for the Spanish Throne' from W. M. Simon (1968) Ger-

many in the Age of Bismarck (George Allen & Unwin) tr. Isabella M. Massey (1957) (London)

(ii) On my return to affairs I learned of the latest negotiations about the candidature for the Spanish throne and cannot resist the impression that in them German interests have not received their
25 due. ... I have once more begged His Majesty the King to reconsider the question ... and received the answer that as soon as any Prince of the House of Hohenzollern showed any inclination to accept the crown he would raise no objection whatever ... the king will certainly never make a decision to *command* a member of
30 the Royal House to undertake a mission the success of which lies predominantly in the sense of *vocation* personally felt by him who undertakes it. ...
     ... If ... one of Your Royal Highness's younger sons were inclined to render service to *both* countries and earn the gratitude of
35 Spain and Germany ... [it] would afford a possibility for me to reopen the question. ...

Bismarck to Prince Karl Anton of Hohenzollern, 28 May 1970, (Ibid, p.158)

(iii) First, I should like to greet you on your arrival in Sigmaringen. This may *perhaps* be the last time you salute your native town and homeland for some while. I have neither the will nor the power to
40 think about it.
     It breaks my heart. Transports of feeling are, however, of no use here. The present day demands realism. The days of ideal attitudes are associated for me with the categorical imperative of the present. ...
45 ... yesterday, I talked for half an hour with the king and Bismarck ... The king is *d'accord* with us, that is, he accommodates himself to the political constraint of Bismarck. The latter triumphs. ... Had we again refused, we should have had to pay for it; for the question of the Spanish throne is a prime factor in Bismarck's
50 political calculations. ... Perhaps some European event or other will yet come to prevent it – if so, all the better.

Prince Karl Anton to his son, Prince Leopold, 5 June 1870, in J. Dittrich (1962) *Bismarck, Frankreich und die Spanische Thronkandidatur der Hohenzollern: Die 'Kriegsschuldfrage' von 1870* (Munich) no. 68, p 394

Questions

a 'French peaceableness towards Germany will always wax or wane in proportion to the dangers of war with Germany' (lines 8–9). Was this so, and, if so, how would a Hohenzollern on the Spanish throne affect this 'peaceableness'?

b 'A rejection of the profferred crown would probably have undesirable consequences' (lines 20–21). What were these and what did
Bismarck not add in this extract which he might have done?

★ c Explain the motive underlying Bismarck's letter to Prince Karl
Anton.

d What is to be understood by 'the sense of *vocation*' (line 31) in
the context in which Bismarck uses it?

e Why might it be Prince Leopold's 'last time' to salute his native
town (line 38)?

f What is to be understood by the 'categorical imperative of the
present' (lines 43–44)?

g Explain Prince Karl Anton's view of the behaviour of the king
in the third extract.

★ h 'Had we again refused, we should have had to pay for it' (line
48). Discuss the significance (and accuracy) of this remark.

3 The Ems despatch

(i) [The original version] *To the Federal Chancellor, Count Bismarck.*
. . . His Majesty the King writes to me:

'M. Benedetti intercepted me on the Promenade in order to
demand of me most insistently that I should authorise him to
5 telegraph immediately to Paris that I shall obligate myself for all
future time never again to give my approval to the candidacy of the
Hohenzollerns should it be renewed. I refused to agree to this, the
last time somewhat severely, informing him that one dare not and
cannot assume such obligations *à tout jamais*. Naturally, I informed
10 him that I had received no news as yet, and since he had been
informed earlier than I by way of Paris and Madrid, he could easily
understand why my government was once again out of the matter.'

Since then His Majesty has received a despatch from the Prince
[Karl Anton]. As His Majesty has informed Count Benedetti that
15 he was expecting news from the Prince, His Majesty himself, in
view of the above-mentioned demand and in consonance with the
advice of Count Eulenburg and myself, decided not to receive the
French envoy but to inform him through an adjutant that His
Majesty had now received from the Prince confirmation of the
20 news which Benedetti had already received from Paris, and that he
had nothing further to say to the ambassador. His Majesty leaves it
to the judgement of Your Excellency whether or not to communicate at once the new demand by Benedetti and its rejection to our
ambassadors and to the press.

[Signed] A[beken] 13.7.70, [Heinrich Abeken was German
Councillor of Legation in Paris], (*Propyläen Weltgeschichte,
Berlin* 1930, vol viii p 248) quoted in L. L. Snyder *op. cit.*

25 (ii) [Bismarck's edited version]

After the reports of the renunciation by the hereditary Prince of Hohenzollern had been officially transmitted by the Royal Government of Spain to the Imperial Government of France, the French ambassador presented to His Majesty the King at Ems the demand
30 to authorise him to telegraph to Paris that His Majesty the King would obligate himself for all future time never again to give his approval to the candidacy of the Hohenzollern should it be renewed.

His Majesty the King thereupon refused to receive the French
35 envoy again and informed him through an adjutant that His Majesty had nothing further to say to the Ambassador.

[Ibid]

(iii) I invited Generals Moltke and Roon to have dinner with me on July 13th, and spoke to them concerning my views and intentions. During the dinner conversation it was reported to me that a code
40 telegram had been received from Ems. ... I ... read it to my guests, who were so crushed that they refused to eat or drink.

All considerations, conscious or unconscious, strengthened my opinion that war could be avoided only at the cost of the honour of Prussia and of the national confidence in her.
45 Under this conviction I made use of the royal authority communicated to me through Abeken to publish the contents of the telegram. In the presence of my guests I reduced the telegram by deleting words but without adding or altering a single word. ...
50 The difference in the effect of the shortened text ... made the announcement appear decisive.

After I had read the condensed version to my two guests, Moltke said: 'Now it has quite a different ring. In its original form, it sounded like a parley. Now it is like a flourish of trumpets in
55 answer to a challenge!'

I went on to explain: 'If ... I immediately communicate this text ... it will be known in Paris before midnight ... it will have the effect of a red flag on the Gallic bull.

'We must fight if we do not want to act the part of the defeated
60 without a battle. However, success depends essentially upon the impression which the beginning of the war makes upon us and others. It is most important that we should be the ones attacked. Gallic insolence and sensitivity will bring this about if we announce before all Europe, as far as we can without the speaking tube of the
65 *Reichstag*, that we are courageously meeting the public threats of France. ...

O. von Bismarck (1898) *Gedanken und Erinnerungen* (Stuttgart and Berlin) II, pp 406–408 *a* Explain (according to the first [Abeken] version of the Ems despatch) the refusal of the king to acede to the demands of Count Benedetti when they met 'on the Promenade' (line 3). What was the significance of that meeting place?

   b From this first version, what does one surmise were the contents of the despatch to Prince Karl Anton (lines 3–12)?

   c Why did the contents of this despatch encourage the king to refuse to receive Count Benedetti?

★ *d* Why was the king proposing to leave the episode in the hands of Bismarck?

   e What is the renunciation referred to in line 26?

   f Explain in detail the critical omissions of the second, amended, text of the Ems despatch. Why was this second version more likely to provoke offence in France?

   g Why were Bismarck's guests 'so crushed' (line 41) by the contents of the telegram?

   h How does Bismarck's concept of 'war' here (line 43) equate with that in the first extract in the first section of this chapter?

   i 'A red flag on the Gallic bull' (line 58). Comment on this use of language and of that of the subsequent paragraph.

   j In what way does the final paragraph of the third extract demonstrate *realpolitik*?

4   A will to unite?

(i) . . . The candidacy of a German prince for the throne of Spain, in the proposal and removal of which all the allied governments had no part, and which was of interest to the North German Confederation only insofar as the government of a friendly nation
5   desired to obtain an orderly and peace-loving régime, has led the government of the French Emperor to war, as the result of a unique diplomatic exchange. . . .

     If Germany in preceding centuries has silently borne such violations of her rights and her honour, it was only because, in her
10 divided condition, she never knew how strong she really was. Today, with a spiritual and legal bond of unity . . . she bears in herself the will and the power to frustrate any new French deeds of violence. . . .

     . . . it is a fact that those in power in France have understood how
15 to utilise for their personal interest the well meaning but excitable temperament of our great neighbouring people.

     The more the allied governments realise how every honourable and dignified method was used to secure the blessings of peace for Europe and how plain it is before all eyes that the sword has been

20   forced into our hands, the more certain we shall be in our call to
defend our honour and independence, fortified as we are in the
unified will of the German governments of both North and South
and in the German people's love for the Fatherland ...

> Throne speech by William I at the opening of an extra-
> ordinary session of the North German *Reichstag*, July 19
> 1870, (*Stenographische Berichte über die Verhandlungen das
> Reichstages*, 1870, 2nd session, pp 1ff)

(ii) From all tribes of the German fatherland, from all circles of the
25 German people, even from across the seas ... I have received so
many messages of devotion ... that it has become imperative that I
recognise publicly the harmony of the German spirit. ... The love
for our common Fatherland and the unanimous uprising of the
German people and their princes have reconciled all differences and
30 opposition. ...

> William I's proclamation '*An das deutsche Volk*', July 25
> 1870, (*Der deutsch-französische Krieg*', Berlin 1872–1881, Pt
> 1, sect 1, p 120)

Questions

a   Comment on William I's description of how Prussia came to be
at war with France.
b   '... a unique diplomatic exchange' (lines 6–7). In what ways is
this a misleading description?
c   What was the 'legal bond of unity' described in line 11?
d   '... those in power in France have understood how to utilise ...
the well-meaning but excitable temperament of our great neighbouring people' (lines 14–16). To what incidents does this refer?
★ e   How can one reconcile William I's bellicose call to arms in the
first extract with his previous timidity over the Hohenzollern
candidature?
f   '... it has become imperative that I recognise publicly the
harmony of the German spirit' (lines 26–27). What, in practical
terms, did that involve?

5 Bismarck during the war: a military observer reports

7 December 1870: Count Bismarck is really beginning to be fit for a
lunatic asylum. ... It is lamentable how inefficient our ministry of
war is. ... General Roon is lazy. ... In the evening a telegram
arrived from Under Secretary von Thile in Berlin in which he
5 reports to Count Bismarck that diplomatic circles in Berlin are
convinced that the government in Paris is only awaiting the

beginning of the bombardment to offer capitulation. This is possible but not likely. It is more plausible that Count Bismarck ordered the telegram in order to lend more weight to the requests
10 for bombardment. . . .

18 December 1870: . . . Count Bismarck has already stressed several times that he must always be kept informed of the course of military events in order to conduct his diplomatic activity accordingly. . . . But if he is informed of intentions, then on the one hand
15 this will invite criticism from a man who is striving after supreme power, including military power. . . . It is contrary to all wellfound usage to discuss operations under way or intended with persons who lack the necessary understanding. . . . But Count Bismarck regards himself as qualified and has already made several
20 attempts to acquire an influence on military operations. . . .

25 January 1871: . . . General Moltke received a command in the King's own handwriting to inform Count Bismarck at once of the military situation in detail. . . . Now, in fact, Count Bismarck receives all reports coming in to us so quickly that he even finds it
25 possible to let the news from the battlefield that he turns over to Reuters in London reach the home country first via this source; they arrive there earlier than our official telegrams. . . .

[Bismarck] . . . I understand is negotiating the capitulation of Paris . . . without General Moltke's opinion being asked before-
30 hand. In view of the lack of military knowledge characteristic of this civilian in a cavalry officer's coat we could therefore easily find ourselves suddenly confronted with a *fait accompli* which is not militarily feasible.

June 1871: . . . The total incompetence and exhaustion of General
35 Roon is generally known, but nobody dares to tell the emperor the truth. . . . Prince Bismarck is certainly the man who is most content with this situation; he could find no more amenable Prussian minister of war than General Roon and in view of his megalomania this is all he needs for the time being. . . .

> From the secret war diary of Lieutenant Colonel Paul
> Bronsart von Schellendorf, 1870–1871, (*Geheimes Kriegsta-*
> *gebuch 1870–71* pp 174 *et passim*) in W. W. Simon *op. cit.*

Questions

★ *a* What evidence is provided here (or exists besides) for the 'lamentable' (line 2) inefficiency of the War Ministry?
   b Why should Bismarck have been anxious to press for a bombardment?
   c '. . . a man who is striving for supreme power' (lines 15–16). How balanced and well informed is such an assessment at this point likely to have been?

    d To what extent do the contents of the entry for 25 January (i) explain Bismarck's unpopularity with the military and (ii) validate the other criticisms made in this extract?

★ *e* Discuss the picture of the king which emerges from these extracts.

6 France surrenders

(i) Sir, My Brother!

    Since I was not able to die in the midst of my troops, it only remains for me to surrender my sword to the hands of Your Majesty.

5   I am, Your Majesty's Good Brother

NAPOLEON

Sedan, 1 September 1870

          Napoleon III to King William I (*Der deutsch-französische Krieg*, Berlin 1872–1881, Pt 1, section 8, p 313)

(ii) Sir, My Brother!

    While regretting the circumstances in which we shall meet, I

10 accept the sword of Your Majesty, and I urge you to grant one of your officers full power to arrange the capitulation of the army that has fought so bravely under your orders. On my side, I have designated General Moltke to that effect.

    I am, Your Majesty's Good Brother

15 WILLIAM

Before Sedan, 1 September 1870

          King William I to Napoleon III (ibid)

(iii) I hastily dressed myself and after I had informed them down-stairs that the Chief had left for Sedan in order to meet the Emperor Napoleon . . . I followed him as quickly as I could. About 800 paces

20 from the bridge across the Meuse at Donchery . . . is a single house.
. . .

    Promptly at eight o'clock, Moltke arrives with a few officers of the general staff, but he leaves again after a short stay. Soon a short, thick-set man, in a red cap with gold lace, and wearing red trousers

25 . . . steps from behind the house and speaks with French officers . . . He wears white kid gloves, and smokes a cigarette. It is the Emperor. I am but a short distance from him, and I can clearly distinguish his features. There is something soft and dreamy in his light grey eyes, which seem like those of people who have lived

30 fast. . . . His whole appearance has something altogether unmilitary about it. The man is too soft. . . . These impressions force them-selves upon one all the more when one looks at the tall, well-set figure of our Chancellor. Napoleon seems tired. . . .

After a pause, he goes over to the Chief, and speaks with him for
35 about three minutes, and then, still smoking ... he walks up and
down the potato garden. A further brief conversation follows
between the Emperor and the Chancellor, begun by Bismarck,
after which Napoleon once more talks with his French suite. About
a quarter to nine, Bismarck and his cousin leave. ... I follow
40 them. ...

The next morning ... as I waded in the drizzling rain ... I met a
long procession of conveyances coming from the Meuse bridge
under the escort of the black death's-head hussars.

In a closed coupé immediately behind the hussars sat the Prisoner
45 of Sedan, the Emperor Napoleon, on his way to Wilhelmshöhe
through Belgium.

> Moritz Busch (1899) in *Tagebuchblätter* (Leipzig) I, pp 153–
> 164 passim quoted in L. L. Snyder *op. cit.*

Questions

★ *a* Is Napoleon III's explanation that he was 'not able to die in the
midst of my troops' (line 2) merely melodrama?

★ *b* '... the army that has fought so bravely under your orders'
(lines 11–12). How true was this? Why anyway were negotiations for the capitulation being conducted by the king?

c Contrast and compare the pictures of Napoleon III and Bismarck which emerge in the last extract.

7   The German Empire becomes a reality

(i) ... As to the basis of these negotiations, I should prefer the
establishment of a close Confederation to any other. The basis is, in
my view, the only one which meets the wishes of the German
nation. It is the only one, therefore, suitable for the foundation of
5   permanent institutions, while it is at the same time sufficient to
assure such a position to Bavaria in the Germanic Confederation, to
which on account of her importance, she has a claim ...

> Bismarck to Bray (new Prime Minister of Bavaria), 4
> November 1870, (O. von Bismarck *Gesammelte Werke*, vol
> vi b, no. 1905, p 580)

(ii) ... We cannot refrain from giving thanks for the joint action
under arms of the whole of Germany. Its efforts transcend the
10 results won on the battlefield and foreshadow the peaceable completion of the work of unification ... we address to His Majesty,
the King of Prussia, the request that it may please him to accept the
Imperial Crown and so consecrate the work of unification. ... The
Confederation shall become a *Reich*, a united and closed state. ...

15   *The President:* ... Thanks to the victories to which Your Majesty
led the armies of Germany in loyal comradeship-in-arms, the
nation now looks forward to permanent unity.

United with the Princes of Germany, the North German *Reichstag*
approaches Your Majesty with the request that it may please Your
20   Majesty by the acceptance of the Imperial Crown of Germany to
consecrate the work of unification. ...

> Report of the sitting of the *Reichstag*, 10 December 1870, in
> K. L. Aegidi *et al.* (eds) (1871) *Das Staatsarchiv, Sammlung
> der offiziellen Aktenstücke der Gegenwart*, no. 20, Dok no.
> 4197, p 55

(iii) ... For three hours, in an overheated room, we [the King of
Prussia, the Crown Prince, Bismarck and von Schleinitz, Minister
of the Household] deliberated on the title of the Emperor, the name
25   for the Crown Prince, the position of the Royal family, the Court
and the army in relation to the *Reich* and so on.

As to the title of the Emperor, Count Bismarck acknowledged
that, in the discussions of the constitution, the Bavarian representatives ... had not wished to permit the designation 'Emperor of
30   Germany', and that he [Bismarck] had finally given way but, of
course, without asking His Majesty first, and conceded the title
'German Emperor'. This designation, with which no real idea is
associated, displeased the King as well as myself ... Count
Bismarck remained firm. Further, he tried to show that the
35   expression 'Emperor of Germany' signified a territorial power such
as we did not in any way possess over the *Reich*. ... So, alas, we
had to submit. This was the occasion for a most painful debate
about the relation of the emperor to king. It arose because His
Majesty, contrary to the old Prussian traditions, placed an emperor
40   higher in dignity than a king. The two ministers and I, with them,
opposed this view extremely clearly. ...

The more clearly ... the consequences of adopting the titles of
'Emperor' and *Reich* became evident, the more enraged the king
became. Finally, he broke out in words to the effect that he was
45   taking on only a shadow empire, nothing more than another
designation for 'President'. ... Now that things had gone so far, he
must bear this cross, but he wished to be the only one to suffer; he
could not, therefore, permit that he should be expected to make the
same demand from the army as from his own person. Therefore,
50   he would not hear of calling it the 'Imperial Army'; he wished to
protect, at least, the Prussian army from such things. He could not
tolerate it that Prussian troops should be asked to accept German
names and designations. The navy might be called the 'Imperial
Navy'. Further, he said in the utmost excitement that he could not
55   describe to us at all how desperate he felt at having to take leave

tomorrow of the old Prussia to which he alone held steadfast, and wished to hold steadfast in the future. Sobs and tears interrupted his words. . . .

> Extract from the Crown Prince's diary, 17 January 1871, in J. Hohfeld (1927) *Deutsche Reichsgeschichte in Dokumenten* vol i, p 69

Questions

a   What did Bismarck understand by 'a close confederation' (line 2) and what evidence is there that this met 'the wishes of the German nation' (lines 3–4)?

★ b   Was the first extract likely to reassure the person to whom it was written? What would have been his especial concerns?

c   What significant developments in the plans for a united Germany appear to have occurred in the interval between the events described in the first and the second extracts?

d   'Count Bismarck remained firm' (lines 33–34). Why was Bismarck apparently in a position to dictate choices to the king?

e   '. . . a territorial power such as we did not in any way possess' (lines 35–36). Was this so, and why in this case were the other states accepting unification?

★ f   Was it tenable to have a Prussian army within a German Empire, as the king desired (lines 38–40)?

g   Was the King's outburst mere petulance or was there justice in his assertion 'that he was taking on only a shadow empire' (lines 44–45)?

★ h   In what ways is the episode described in the third extract reminiscent of events in 1848?

8   Looking to the future

(i) There is a new element in politics, a deepening, of which earlier victors knew nothing or at least made no conscious use. One is trying to humiliate the loser as much as possible, so that in the future he will hardly dare to move. It is possible that this aim will
5   be achieved; but whether one's own position will be the better and happier as a result is another question altogether.

Oh how the German nation errs if it thinks it will be able to put the rifle in one corner and turn to the arts and the happiness of peace! They will be told; above all you must continue your military
10   training! And after a time no one will really be able to say what is the purpose of living. For soon the German–Russian war will loom on the horizon. . . .

> Jacob Burckhardt (1963) *Briefe*, Basel-Stuttgart Vol 5, pp 111 ff quoted in J. C. G. Röhl (1970) *From Bismarck to Hitler* (Longman)

(ii) ... Now let me impress upon the attention of the House the
character of this war. It is no common war, like the war between
15 Austria and Prussia, or like the Italian war in which France was
engaged some years ago; nor is it like the Crimean War. This war
represents the German Revolution, a greater political event than the
French Revolution last century – I don't say a greater, or as great,
social event. What its social consequences may be are in the future.
20 Not a single principle in the management of our foreign affairs,
accepted by all statesmen for guidance up to six months ago, any
longer exists, there is not a diplomatic tradition which has not been
swept away. You have a new world, new influences at work, new
and unknown objects and dangers with which to cope, at present
25 involved in that obscurity incident to novelty in such affairs. We
used to have discussions in this House about the balance of power.
... The balance of power has been entirely destroyed. ...

> Benjamin Disraeli in the House of Commons, 9 February
> 1871 (Hansard, Series III, Vol CCIV, February–March
> 1871, pp 81 ff) quoted in J. C. G. Röhl (ibid)

Questions

★ *a* 'a new element ... is trying to humiliate the loser as much as
possible' (lines 1–3). How true was this of Prussia's treatment of
France after her defeat?

★ *b* In what ways was Burckhardt's warning prescient? Why did he
fear especially a Germano-Russian war?

c What is one to understand of Disraeli's description of 'a
common war' (line 14)?

d 'The balance of power has been entirely destroyed' (line 27).
Was this merely political hyperbole?